P9-DBN-806

Dynamics of Office Markets

JOHN M. CLAPP

with commentary by
Michael Raper and
Keith R. Ihlanfeldt
and by
Kenneth T. Rosen

DYNAMICS OF OFFICE MARKETS

Empirical Findings and Research Issues

AREUEA Monograph Series, No. 1

THE URBAN INSTITUTE PRESS
Washington, D.C.

THE URBAN INSTITUTE PRESS
2100 M Street, N.W.
Washington, D.C. 20037

Editorial Advisory Board

William Gorham
Craig G. Coelen
Adele V. Harrell
Ronald B. Mincy
Marilyn Moon

Demetra S. Nightingale
George E. Peterson
Felicity Skidmore
Raymond J. Struyk

Copyright © 1993. The Urban Institute. All rights reserved. Except for short quotes, no part of this book may be reproduced or utilized in any form or by any means, electronic or mechanical, including photocopying, recording, or by information storage or retrieval system, without written permission from The Urban Institute Press.

Library of Congress Cataloging in Publication Data

Clapp, John M.
    Dynamics of office markets : empirical findings and research issues / by John M. Clapp ; with comments by Michael Raper and Keith Ihlanfeldt and by Kenneth T. Rosen.
        p. cm.—(AREUEA monographs)

    Includes bibliographical references and index.
    1. Offices—Location.   2. Office buildings.   I. Title. II. Series.

HF5547.25.C58   1993   93.21571
658.2'1—dc20   CIP

    ISBN 0-87766-606-7 (alk. paper)
    ISBN 0-87766-605-9 (alk. paper; casebound)

Urban Institute books are printed on acid-free paper whenever possible.

Printed in the United States of America.

Distributed by University Press of America

4720 Boston Way
Lanham, MD 20706

3 Henrietta Street
London WC2E 8LU ENGLAND

THE URBAN INSTITUTE
Board of Trustees
David O. Maxwell
  Chairman
Katharine Graham
  Vice Chairman
William Gorham
  President
Angela Glover Blackwell
Joan Toland Bok
James E. Burke
Marcia L. Carsey
Carol Thompson Cole
Richard B. Fisher
George J.W. Goodman
Richard C. Green, Jr.
Fernando A. Guerra, M.D.
Ruth Simms Hamilton
Carla A. Hills
Reuben Mark
Ann McLaughlin
Robert S. McNamara
Charles L. Mee, Jr.
Robert C. Miller
Franklin D. Raines

AREUEA
Board of Directors
Mike Miles
  President
Austin J. Jaffee
  First Vice President
Peter F. Colwell
  Second Vice President
John L. Glascock
  Secretary-Treasurer
Jan K. Brueckner
Dennis Capozza
John M. Clapp
Jeffrey D. Fisher
Stuart Gabriel
Michael Giliberto
Jack Harris
Donald R. Haurin
David Ling
Edwin Mills
Henry O. Pollakowski
J. Sa-Aadu
James D. Shilling
C.F. Sirmans
John Tuccillo
Kerry D. Vandell
Michelle J. White
Peter M. Zorn

The Urban Institute Press is a refereed press. Its Editorial Advisory Board makes publication decisions on the basis of referee reports solicited from recognized experts in the field. Established and supported by The Urban Institute, the Press disseminates policy research on important social and economic problems, not only by Institute staff but also by outside authors.

The Dynamics of Office Markets: Empirical Findings and Research Issues, by John M. Clapp, is an AREUEA Monograph.

Conclusions are those of the authors and do not necessarily reflect the views of staff members, officers, trustees, advisory groups, or funders of The Urban Institute or The American Real Estate and Urban Economics Association.

ACKNOWLEDGMENTS

I would like to thank the Series Editor, Anthony Yezer, for his careful reading of at least two earlier drafts of this monograph. His comments and suggestions have been invaluable.

My interest in office markets, begun under the tutelage of Frank Mittelbach at UCLA, was nourished by a series of seminars held at the Homer Hoyt Institute, Weimer School of Advanced Studies in Florida. Also, HHI has contributed funding to assist numerous studies of the office market, many of which appeared in a special issue of the *AREUEA Journal* edited by Henry Pollakowski. My participation in that special issue was certainly the catalyst that made this monograph possible.

The Center for Real Estate and Urban Economic Studies (CREUES) at the University of Connecticut has been an important source of assistance in the production of this monograph. CREUES provided research assistance, editorial assistance and especially expert secretarial help. The Urban Institute provided an excellent editing job.

On a personal level, my children Jeremy and Corey have been a great source of comfort and joy during the period when this monograph was written. My friends Al Rosa and Candy Bianco have provided understanding and a willingness to accommodate my busy schedule.

CONTENTS

viii   *Contents*

Tables

Figures

FOREWORD

The Urban Institute's commitment to studying urban problems and strategies to alleviate them is reflected in the central role urban economists have always played in the Institute's own work. Duncan MacRae, Robert Buckley, and James Follain are all Institute alumni. George Peterson and Raymond Struyk are among the urban economists currently on staff.

The importance we attach to urban economics (including real estate economics) as an analytic lens for studying the city's characteristics and problems, and the impacts of public policy on them, makes the Institute a most appropriate publisher for the new Monograph Series sponsored by the American Real Estate and Urban Economics Association (AREUEA).

The intent of the AREUEA series is to summarize and synthesize recent research developments in an easily accessible form—for use by teachers, students, and practitioners (including urban planners, real estate investors, appraisers, the housing policy community, home and commercial builders, and the real estate finance industry).

The topic of this first AREUEA monograph—the dynamics of office markets—is particularly timely given the boom-bust pattern of office construction over the past decade or so, and its destructive effects on city economies. The author's central question is: How should lenders, investors, developers, and other real estate professionals (public and private) change the way they make decisions to avoid such cycles in the future? In addressing it, he not only reviews recent research developments in the main line real estate economics literature. He also uses techniques from geography, and more qualitative institutional evidence on how markets function, in an effort to illuminate behavioral differences among office users—for example, small versus large businesses, branch versus main offices, businesses for which employee preferences are important versus businesses for which they may not be a factor.

I expect this book to be helpful to the teachers, students, and practitioners for whom it is written, and to provide reliable guidance to those responsible for office building decisions. Smoothing office building cycles will not only benefit lenders, investors, and developers. It should also increase the stability of the wider economic environment facing city residents and city governments.

William Gorham
President

Chapter One

INTRODUCTION

This monograph critically reviews the empirical literature on office markets, including studies pertaining to the demand or supply of office space (e.g., square footage and building permits), spatial or temporal patterns of office employment, and office market conditions (e.g., vacancy and rental rates).[1] The work cited comes primarily from geography and economics, with some contributions from planning and allied disciplines.

This analysis provides useful perspective to real estate practitioners on the painful experiences of the 1980s and early 1990s. Many lenders, investors, and developers have been shocked and dispirited by declining office rents, high vacancy rates, and huge declines in property values. Many now face a quandary: should they sell office properties that remain in their portfolio, or should they buy on the expectation that we are now at the bottom of the cycle? Furthermore, when office markets do improve, how should lenders, investors, developers, and other real estate professionals change the way they make decisions? The analyses included here—especially those in chapters 2, 3, and 7—suggest some answers to these questions.

This monograph provides supplementary material for graduate- and undergraduate-level courses in real estate, urban economics, and geography. In nontechnical language, it describes numerous facets of the market for office space. Courses with a strong theoretical base will want to focus on chapters 2 through 5; urban economics courses will find chapters 2 and 3 especially useful; and geography courses will find chapters 4 and 5 particularly helpful. Courses with more of an applied orientation will want to concentrate on chapters 1, 3, 6, and 7. Finally, the contributions at the end of this volume by Raper and Ihlanfeldt and by Rosen will be useful in courses in urban economics and geography (Raper and Ihlanfeldt) and real estate (Rosen).

The scope of this monograph is restricted to studies explicitly directed to office markets. Literature is excluded that focuses primarily on urban or regional trends, or on general descriptions of the service sector, even when dealing with office markets tangentially. For example, in reference to Noyelle and Stanbach, Jr.'s 1984 study, their typology of cities is not considered here, but their discussion of employment in the finance, insurance, and services sectors is. Likewise, whereas Daniels (1979) reviewed some of the office market literature and related it to trends in the service sector, only his discussion of office markets is addressed here.

SIGNIFICANCE OF OFFICE MARKETS

The importance of office markets research is underscored by the rapid growth of employment in industries using a substantial amount of office space (see definition of office activity in the next section). I begin by reviewing literature on the importance of the office market.

Nearly 90 percent of total U.S. employment growth between 1970 and 1980 was in industries that use a considerable amount of office space. Office employment (i.e., jobs located in office space) grew by about 5 million over the decade compared to total nonagricultural employment growth of 21 million (i.e., office space housed nearly one-quarter of all new workers from 1970 to 1980) (see Noyelle and Stanback, Jr. 1984). Noyelle and Stanback, Jr., showed that the pattern in the 1970s was a continuation of long-term post–World War II structural shifts in the economy.[2] In the largest urban areas, expansion during the 1970s was slower, with office space growing about 38 percent, office employment growing by 21 percent, and total employment in office-using industries growing by 21 percent (1.9 percent per year) (Wheaton and Torto 1985).[3]

In the 1980s, office employment grew by about 5.1 million, whereas total nonagricultural employment grew by only 19 million people; thus, office space housed about 27 percent of all new workers (see Rosen's commentary at the end of this volume). In comparison to the 1970s, employment growth rates during the 1980s declined (both total and in office space), but office employment growth was more important relative to total employment growth. Rosen (see end of this volume) estimates that employment growth housed in office space will account for about 23 percent of total employment growth from 1990 through the year 2000. Therefore, according to his projec-

Figure 1.1 ANNUAL CHANGE IN EMPLOYMENT, BY INDUSTRY, IN NINE U.S. CITIES: 1969–89

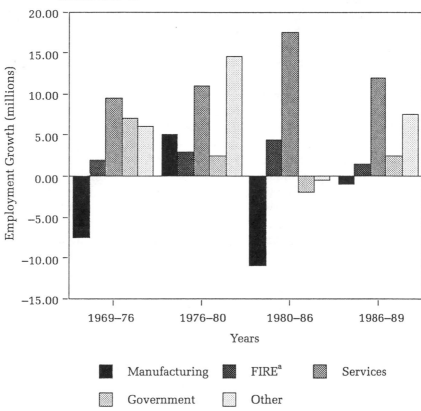

Notes: The nine cities are: Anaheim, Atlanta, Boston, Chicago, Dallas, Houston, Los Angeles, New York, and Philadelphia. Even though the figure is divided into six-year and three-year periods, the data are for annual changes, so the bars from one time period can be compared to those for another. The "Other" category is largely wholesale and retail trade, as well as transportation, communications, and utilities; it is *not* a major office-using sector.
a. FIRE: finance, insurance, and real estate.

tions, the slower rates of employment growth during the 1990s will be accompanied by a return to the relative growth rates of the 1970s.

Figure 1.1 presents employment by industry for 1969 to 1989. In the nine major metropolitan areas included in the figure, manufacturing employment declined over most of this period. Growth in government employment, a major office-using sector, was high in the 1970s but slowed considerably in the 1980s. Thus, one source of growth in demand for office space has recently disappeared or become much less important.

The major sources of demand for office space are in the FIRE (finance, insurance, real estate) and services industries, which together comprise the majority of office employment. FIRE employment grew throughout 1969–89, and most strongly during 1976–86. Service industries (about 40 percent of employment uses office space) were the strongest growth sector, especially during 1980–86. Thus, office employment growth has clearly been a major longtime contributor to economic growth in the United States.

Because of its linkages to other sectors of the economy, office employment has been a driving force in the development of metropolitan, state, and regional economies. State and local officials responsible for planning and economic development have been eager to attract office employment. This is particularly true because of the linkages among office activities. For example, regional headquarters need ancillary services such as accounting, legal, financial, and marketing expertise. Hence, growth in one part of the office sector stimulates growth throughout the sector. This, in turn, stimulates growth in the entire economy, including service-sector jobs such as retailing and food service jobs. Planning officials aware of this have promoted growth of office employment to invigorate the entire local and regional economy.

By the same token, when office employment slumps, the demand for related services—such as secretarial agencies, courier services, and legal and accounting services—also decreases. The demand for all the retail goods and services that office employees typically buy furthermore declines. Thus, the entire metropolitan economy will suffer because of the reduction in office employment.

Office employment growth provides a particularly desirable means to stimulate local economies, especially the city centers and their associated suburbs. Compared to the production of goods, office activities typically do less damage to the environment. Furthermore, they generate more tax revenue per employee because the employees have higher incomes than factory workers.

Because of declines in many office markets in recent years, investors and lenders are considerably more cautious about the market for existing or new office buildings. However, memories are short, and strictures will relax as the market recovers. Therefore, those interested in improving the accuracy of supply-demand models of the office market need to move quickly to take advantage of the current interest in improved analysis.

DEFINING OFFICE EMPLOYMENT AND OFFICE ACTIVITY

Office employment is concentrated in finance, insurance, and real estate (FIRE); business, professional, and legal services; government; central administrative offices and auxiliary establishments of manufacturing firms; consumer services (lodging, personal repair services, amusement, recreation, and private household services); health services; social services; and membership organizations. It is useful to consider differences between office employment and other employment in trade (retail and wholesale), distributive services (transportation, communications, and utilities), and educational services.

Office activity is difficult to define, partly because office work is performed by managerial, technical, professional, and clerical occupations that cut across industrial classifications.[4] Rhodes and Kan (1971) argued that "office functions are concerned with the collecting of information, decision making, the processing of paper work and the administration of other forms of economic activity" (p. 5). All office employees use desks for information processing (the office worker is a desk-using animal); here, "desk" includes the computer console and drafting board, but not the cash register. These concepts clearly distinguish office employment, office space, and other office activities from materials processing, storage of goods, retailing functions, and other activities not in the office sector. Thus, the Rhodes and Kan definition, elaborated by the desk-using concept, provides conceptual boundaries for this study.

PATTERNS OF U.S. OFFICE MARKET GROWTH

As illustrated in figure 1.1 and emphasized earlier, office employment growth has been an integral part of economic growth in the United States over a substantial time period. Office employment has also been essential to the growth of regional and metropolitan economies. In fact, the economic health of various regions can be understood in terms of growth of the office sector. Figures 1.2 and 1.3 examine two regions respectively: the Snowbelt, composed of Boston, Chicago, New York, and Philadelphia; and the Sunbelt, composed of Anaheim, Atlanta, Dallas, Houston, and Los Angeles. Note that the Snowbelt metropolitan areas are primarily the older eastern cities, whereas the Sunbelt contains the newer southern and southwestern cities. The

Figure 1.2 EMPLOYMENT IN SNOWBELT CITIES IN UNITED STATES:
INDUSTRY EMPLOYMENT TO TOTAL SNOWBELT EMPLOYMENT,
1969–89

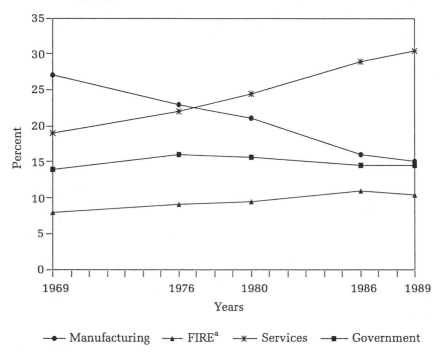

—●— Manufacturing   —▲— FIRE[a]   —*— Services   —■— Government

Note: Snowbelt cities are Boston, Chicago, New York, and Philadelphia.
a. FIRE, finance, insurance, and real estate.

older metropolitan areas in the Snowbelt are generally considerably larger than the newer cities in the Sunbelt.

Figures 1.2 and 1.3 show that manufacturing has declined as a percentage of total employment in both the Snowbelt and Sunbelt, with a particularly rapid drop-off in the Snowbelt. The most important segment of office employment, the FIRE sector, grew relative to total employment in both regions, but more rapidly so in the Sunbelt. A similar story holds for the large services sector. On the other hand, government employment remained about constant as a share of total employment in both regions.

Figure 1.4 shows the relative growth of the Snowbelt and Sunbelt. In 1969, average employment in Snowbelt cities was about 50 percent larger than the average of all nine cities; by 1989, this percentage had declined to about 30 percent. The biggest change was in the

Figure 1.3 EMPLOYMENT IN SUNBELT CITIES IN UNITED STATES: INDUSTRY EMPLOYMENT TO TOTAL SUNBELT EMPLOYMENT, 1969–89

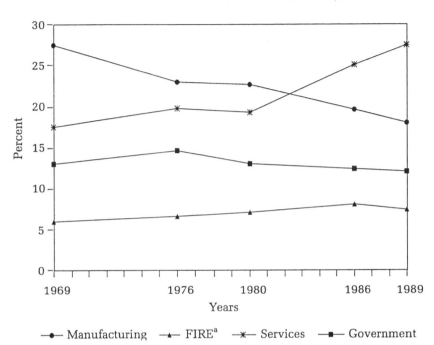

Note: Sunbelt cities are Anaheim, Atlanta, Dallas, Houston, and Los Angeles.
a. FIRE, finance, insurance, and real estate.

manufacturing sector as plants migrated to the lower costs and better working conditions associated with the Sunbelt. Turning to office employment, the services sector (about 40 percent office using) showed the largest shift to the Sunbelt (see figure 1.4). On the other hand, FIRE (about 100 percent office using) showed the least movement to the Sunbelt. It is reasonable to conclude that the Snowbelt remains relatively competitive for the higher-level office jobs that command and control many other sectors (e.g., headquarter jobs).

A major implication of figure 1.4 is that Sunbelt cities enjoyed faster growth of office employment than Snowbelt cities. Therefore, the share of office employment in Snowbelt cities has decreased. Furthermore, the faster growth of Sunbelt cities held throughout the 1980s, despite economic difficulties associated with a fall in oil prices during the early to mid-1980s.

The shift in office growth toward the Sunbelt should not be inter-

Figure 1.4 RELATIVE EMPLOYMENT IN SNOWBELT AND SUNBELT CITIES IN
UNITED STATES: 1969–89

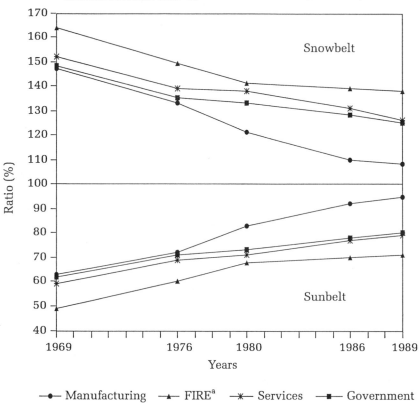

Note: Ratios were calculated by dividing the mean industry employment of the Snowbelt (or Sunbelt) cities (listed in note to figure 1.1) by the mean for all nine cities.
a. FIRE, finance, insurance, and real estate.

preted to mean there was a decline in office employment in major
Snowbelt cities. On the contrary, many of these cities continued to
enjoy positive growth in office employment. For some Snowbelt
cities, all of the positive net growth in employment during the 1980s
came from office and service sector employment (i.e., manufacturing
and related employment declined).

Figure 1.5 illustrates the importance of office employment to the
economic health of Snowbelt cities. If the three major office-using
sectors (FIRE, government, and services) are added together, then
there was substantial net positive growth in employment in each of
the subperiods from 1969 to 1989. On the other hand, manufacturing

Figure 1.5 ANNUAL CHANGE IN EMPLOYMENT IN SNOWBELT CITIES IN
UNITED STATES: 1969–89

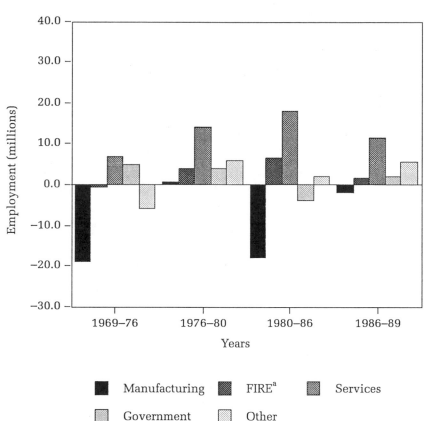

Note: Snowbelt cities are Boston, Chicago, New York, and Philadelphia.
a. FIRE, finance, insurance, and real estate.

employment was constant or declining in each of these subperiods.
Other employment, mainly retail and wholesale trade, does not generally have a role as an engine of growth (see chapter 3); usually this
sector is dependent on export industries such as office activities and
manufacturing employment that fuel growth in the local economy.

Sunbelt cities had positive growth in manufacturing employment
except for the subperiod from 1980 to 1986 (figure 1.6). In addition,
these cities had strongly growing office employment. Other employment followed office and manufacturing employment, typically
growing vigorously over the 20-year period.

Figure 1.6 ANNUAL CHANGE IN EMPLOYMENT IN SUNBELT CITIES IN
UNITED STATES: 1969–89

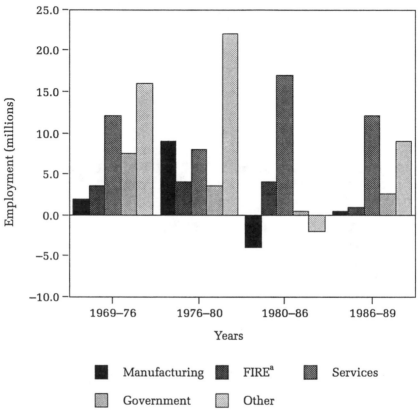

Note: Sunbelt cities are Anaheim, Atlanta, Dallas, Houston, and Los Angeles.
a. FIRE, finance, insurance, and real estate.

Patterns over Time and within Cities

Office markets are characterized by pronounced cycles as rents,
vacancy rates, and construction move up and down. As part of their
analysis of major components of the office market, chapters 2 and 3
examine these factors in more detail, from long construction lags
and unpredictable shifts in demand to "overbuilding" caused by
government policy.

Office employment is particularly important in the central cities
of metropolitan areas because there is virtually no production of

goods in these city centers. However, suburban office markets are growing faster than those of central cities. The suburbanization of office employment and space is discussed in greater detail in chapters 4 and 5.

ACTORS IN THE OFFICE MARKET

Offices are financed, built, leased, owned, and managed because the various participants find it in their self-interest to engage in these activities. Interactions among these participants are explored throughout this book. This section provides an overview of the process that makes office markets work. It also begins to explore the office market at the level of the actors who are most immediately involved with the building's operation.

Figure 1.7 indicates the roles of the various participants in the office market. It is organized around the specific office building, which is at the center of the decisions made by these actors.[5] The figure begins with a specific site and shows how the time and energy of developers, architects, construction contractors, investors, lenders, and associated professionals cause the construction of an office building. Interaction with public officials, notably planning and zoning officials, is a major part of the development of a new office building.

For example, suppose that a developer perceives the need for a new office building at a particular location. The developer would either buy the land or, more likely, obtain an option to buy the land after all approvals have been obtained from the local government. The developer might do a market analysis to evaluate the supply of competing property and the demand for office space in the local area. If the results from the market analysis were favorable, the developer would hire an architect; negotiations and contracts with suppliers and construction contractors would follow. Most importantly, the developer would have to obtain construction permits and other approvals from the local government as well as financing from investors and lenders. Only when these many hurdles were successfully overcome could the developer sign final contracts and begin construction.

Once the building exists, the major actors are the public sector, the building owner, and the tenants. Professionals related to these major players include the tax assessor, the building manager, and the leasing agent. On the demand side are the tenants and certain

Figure 1.7 ROLES OF OFFICE MARKET PARTICIPANTS AND THE SITE

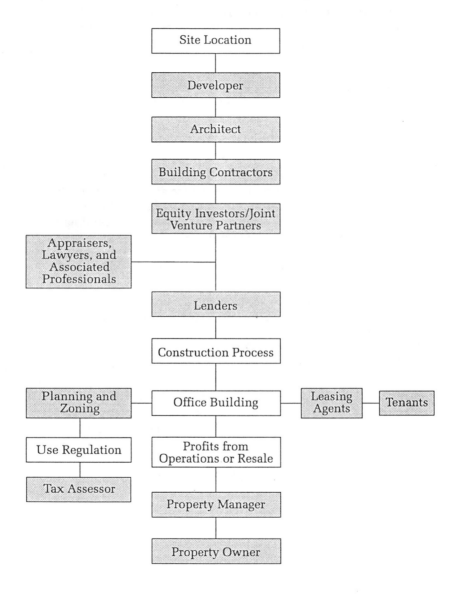

Note: Shaded boxes indicate participation in the office market. Nonshaded boxes indicate a physical location or process.

public officials (e.g., those involved with community development programs). Thus, the actors in the real estate process can be summarized in terms of their relationships to demand and supply. The quest of these actors for profitable opportunities is the engine that drives office markets.

Also on the demand side, rental income to a particular building ultimately derives from the office workers whose employers seek space in that building. (Trends in employment in the office sector have already been reviewed here—see figure 1.1.) Since demand depends on location and building quality, I turn now to building quality.

DEFINING OFFICE SPACE QUALITY

Technology has changed the character of office buildings. Newer office buildings can be built with improved elevators, wiring designed to handle data processing needs, computer hardware designed to control the heating and cooling systems, fiber-optic wires, and facilities to communicate via satellite. Thus, building age is an important factor in determining building quality: "smart buildings" have become a reality.

Office buildings are usually classified as A, B, or C. However, no generally accepted industry standard exists for this classification. Each leasing agent typically develops his or her own standards, and real estate appraisers may have different views of a particular building. One source (Farley Company 1990) defines these classes as follows:

Class A buildings include buildings constructed after 1960.

Class B buildings include buildings constructed between 1940 and 1960, as well as those constructed prior to 1940 that have undergone major renovation and rehabilitation.

Class C buildings include buildings constructed prior to 1940 that have not been significantly renovated.

Cushman & Wakefield (1991) has a more general classification scheme. The firm defines class A buildings as those that are "well located, professionally managed, attract high-quality tenants and command upper-tier rental rates. Structures are modern with high finish or have been modernized to successfully compete with newer buildings." Because of the judgment required in defining office building class, it is often best to rely on classification by a real estate appraiser—presumably, one who is not influenced by the desire to rent a particular building.

CHARACTERISTICS OF THE OFFICE LEASE

The office lease is a lengthy, complex legal document with a number of clauses that strongly influence the dollar value of the lease to the landlord and the cost of the lease to the tenant. Therefore, the terms of the office lease are subject to intense negotiation between landlord and tenant. Major characteristics influencing dollar value include: (1) base rent; (2) the term (e.g., in years) of the lease; (3) provisions for increases in rent; (4) specifications for finishing the leased space (tenant improvements).

Base Rent, Term of Lease, and Related Provisions

Base rent is specified in terms of dollars per year per square foot of occupied space. Tenants occupying part of a floor are generally charged for common areas (halls and elevator lobbies), based on the percentage of the floor that they occupy. The cash payments made on the base rent are modified by free rent. Commonly, landlords attract tenants by making the first few months (generally, one month up to one year) free of charge. A tenant receiving substantial free rent might be willing to pay higher base rental rates; these higher payments would be delayed until after the period of free rent. Alternatively, the tenant might trade off other lease provisions (e.g., higher security deposits for more free rent).

Landlords attempt to attract creditworthy tenants, but they need to charge higher base rents to tenants who might have difficulty meeting their obligations under the lease. Benjamin, Shilling, and Sirmans (1992) have argued that office landlords use differential security deposits to sort out the different types of tenants. Specifically, they have found that a larger security deposit is associated with lower rental obligations under the lease, and that the reduction in rent is greater than the interest forgone on the security deposit. Thus, it appears that landlords can (and do) offer different combinations of security deposit and rental payments to separate tenants by quality. Future research will need to determine whether this is a complete separation or only an imperfect one.

The term of the lease is the number of years or months covered by the lease. Over the past 20 years the term of a typical lease has shortened from 10 to 15 years to about 5 years as of 1992. This probably reflects the rapid growth of smaller, less-secure office tenants, as well as lower rates of inflation.

Benjamin, Sa-Aadu, and Shilling (1992) examined one of the many other provisions of an office market lease, the relocation provision. If the relocation clause is included in the lease, the landlord has the right to relocate tenants to comparable space within the building prior to expiration of the lease contract.[6] This clause gives the landlord the option to reconfigure the building to suit the needs of a major new tenant. Benjamin and colleagues analyzed whether sample selectivity influences attempts to measure the significance of the relocation provision. Sample selectivity arises because only certain office landlords have need for a relocation provision in the office lease. Thus, negotiations on this provision are a factor in only a subset of office leases. Attempts to model office leases that ignore sample selectivity may mistakenly conclude that the relocation provision is not significant when, in fact, it is significant to a subset of the market.

High vacancy rates in the early 1990s provided tenants with enormous bargaining power which they have used, in part, to write more flexible leases (Graham and Giliberto 1993). Tenants may obtain the right to reduce the amount of space that they occupy, or even cancel the lease altogether.[7] Thus, if the tenants' business declines, they have the ability to reduce expenses associated with the lease. Likewise, tenants may obtain the right to expand into adjacent space. When landlords agree to this, they cannot rent this adjacent space for long periods of time without the right to evict with short notice.

Graham and Giliberto (1993) develop the implications of flexible lease terms for landlords and lenders. For example, the contraction option increases a landlord's vacancy risk and makes releasing of smaller areas more difficult. Lenders will discount the value of leases with contraction options, so it is more difficult to refinance buildings with these leases.

Provisions for Rental Increases

Provisions for rental increases over time take many forms. Some leases are written on a gross basis whereby the rent includes taxes, utilities, and maintenance (including insurance). Other leases are written on a "triple net" basis whereby the tenant pays all expenses on a per-square-foot basis. Net leases provide for increases in rent to be paid by tenants as expenses increase. Regardless of whether the lease is net or gross, it may contain a provision for periodic increases called "bumps." Moreover, office rents commonly increase by some fraction of the increase in the consumer price index (CPI).

In a third type of lease, the landlord pays some expenses and the tenants pay others (e.g., not uncommonly, the tenants pay utilities and the landlord pays insurance, at least up to some given dollar amount per square foot—the "stop" clause). Such clauses state that the landlord is responsible for expenses up to the dollar amount of the stop. If expenses rise above the stop, tenants are responsible for the excess amount.

Tenant Improvement (TI) Work Letters

Plans to prepare office space to suit the needs of a particular tenant are an important part of the lease agreement. These "tenant improvements (TIs)" include carpeting, the placement of partitions, wall coverings, ceiling fixtures, and, possibly, special wiring or fiber-optic connections.

Landlords pay for tenant improvements, typically executing a "work letter" specifying exactly what will be done. The amounts involved are typically between $10 and $20 per square foot but can go as high as $40 a square foot. Since an entire year of rental income can be used as TI, the amount involved is a matter of intense negotiation between landlord and tenant.[8] In addition to TI, landlords may pay the expenses for tenants to move into the building ("moving allowances").

Using Rental Rates for Analysis

Because of the complexity of the rental contract, it is very difficult to use rental rates to analyze office markets. One approach is to use quoted rental rates (asking rents), which make no allowance for free rent, TI, moving allowances, or escalation clauses. Asking rents can be stated on a net or gross basis and are often stated as a range. Analysis has been done on asking rents for an entire metropolitan area; in this case, an average asking rent or the midpoint of the range is typically used.

Analysis of office rents can be performed at the building level or at the lease level. At the building level, it is typical to use quoted rents, whereas at the lease level it is more common to use the concept of effective rents or "net effective rents." The effective rental rate has been defined in the industry literature as "actual rental costs including all concessions which result in the actual rate a tenant pays to lease space" (Farley Company 1990). The problem with this definition is that escalation clauses occur in the future, and one must determine how to allocate free rent over the term of the lease. Recently, Wheaton and Torto (1992) defined net effective rent as "the present discounted value of all payments-minus-expenses actually received by the landlord during the term of the lease" (p. 5). The value of tenant improvements and the amount of free rent is subtracted when doing these present-value calculations.

Another concept of rent used by Wheaton and Torto (1992) is "consideration rent," the average rent (not discounted to present value) per square foot per year paid over the term of the lease. It includes escalation clauses and free rent, but not the cost of tenant improvements. Consideration rent represents the average cost of a square foot of space to the tenant, not the net rent received by the landlord.[9]

In a pair of papers, Fisher and Webb (1993) and Webb and Fisher (1993) show how data on leases can be used to construct an index of effective rents. Fisher and Webb (1993) develop a national effective rent index that allows for differences in location, building quality, length (term) of the lease, and TI. They argue that their index is a leading indicator of changes in cash flows and building values.

Webb and Fisher (1993) use more complete data for Chicago to show that a new lease typically involved less rent than renegotiation or renewal of an existing lease. Furthermore, the involvement of a broker reduced effective rent over their sample period (1988–91).[10] More importantly, they develop a data collection form that could be the basis for adding data on additional leases.

Given the amount of rental income, the profitability to office developers and owners depends on their ability to control expenses. Thus, the next section analyzes the expenses associated with operating an office building. Profitability is then examined in terms of growth of expenses relative to growth of rental income.

INCOME AND EXPENSES FOR OFFICE BUILDINGS

This part of the chapter deals with the institutional structure of office markets by examining historical patterns of income and expenses for a typical office building in the United States. All of the information in this section comes from data supplied by the Building Owners and Managers Association (BOMA).[11]

Almost all income received by the owner of an office building comes from rent, including rental of parking spaces. Decisions about investment or lending on office buildings usually begin with potential gross income (PGI), the income that could be earned if the office building were fully rented at current market rents. An estimate of normal vacancy rates is subtracted from PGI to get effective gross income (EGI), that is, the income that would likely be collected at current market rents.

Office markets are characterized by long leases typically ranging from 3 to 15 years in length. This means that the actual rents collected by an existing office building with leases written years in the past can differ substantially from EGI. The data presented in this section are for actual rents collected and actual operating expenses for a typical office building in the BOMA sample. Historical patterns experienced by landlords over this period are also explored. The implications of this for investment and lending decisions, as well as for other real estate decisions, are addressed later in this book.

Figure 1.8 presents a breakdown of office expenses. Total operating expenses were about $10.25 per square foot per year for the typical office building in 1990. The figure shows various categories of office expenses as a percentage of this total (note that financing expenses are not included in the figure). Fixed operating expenses, including real estate taxes and property insurance, were 29 percent of the total. Utilities—including electricity, oil, gas, and telephone—were another 18 percent of cost. Smaller expenses categories such as leasing, repairs, cleaning, security, grounds, and administration, totaled about 53 percent of all operating expenses.

Real estate decisions require an evaluation of trends in office building income and expenses. For example, if expenses are rising much faster than income, then an investor in an office building would expect declining returns on invested capital. Figure 1.9 displays historical trends for rental income and operating expenses for a constant group of office buildings. The most important lines in the figure are the total dollar amount of rent collected per square foot (lines connecting the dots), net operating income (NOI—the line connecting the triangles), and variable operating expenses (utilities, repairs, cleaning, administration, and roads—in figure 1.9, the line connecting the asterisks). Variable expenses grew from 1980 through 1990,

Figure 1.8 MAJOR EXPENSES IN OFFICE BUILDINGS: U.S. PRIVATE SECTOR, PERCENTAGE OF TOTAL

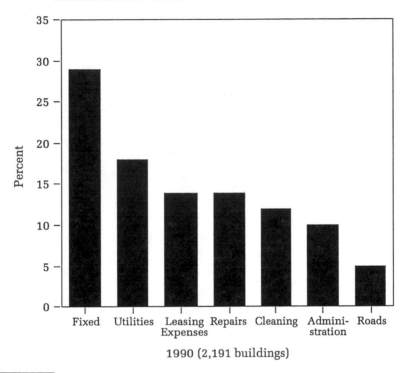

1990 (2,191 buildings)

Note: Figure does not include financing expenses.

but not so rapidly as real estate taxes, insurance, and leasing expenses over the period.

The rental rate per square foot rose faster than variable and fixed operating expenses through 1983, so NOI rose faster than total operating expenses (see figure 1.9). From 1983 through 1990, the rental rate and NOI grew at about the same rate as expenses. Much of the growth in operating expenses during this latter period was caused by relatively rapid increases in fixed operating expenses. Thus, property taxes and insurance grew faster than other expense categories from 1983 through 1990.

Figure 1.9 indicates that landlords experienced some growth in NOI, but that this growth was less rapid over the last eight years of data (1983–90). Thus, landlords were "squeezed" by relatively rapid growth in expenses. When inflation, as measured by the CPI, is com-

Figure 1.9 NOMINAL RENTAL RATE, EXPENSES, AND CONSUMER PRICE INDEX FOR TYPICAL U.S. OFFICE BUILDING: 1973–90

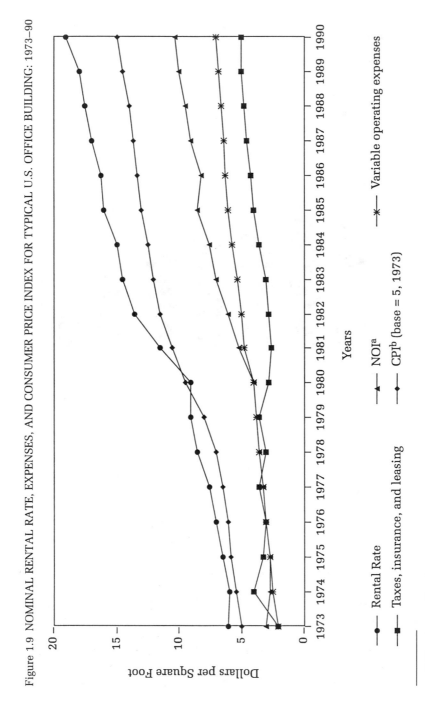

a. NOI, net operating income.
b. CPI, consumer price index.

pared to NOI, one can see that landlords were able to buy less with NOI in 1990 than they could buy in 1983.

Figure 1.9 shows that rent grew at about the same rate as inflation from 1973 through 1980. From 1980 through 1985, rent grew more rapidly than the CPI. From 1985 through 1990, rent grew at about the same rate as the CPI, and during part of the period, more slowly.

The implications of this for the owner of a *new* building are considered in chapter 6 of this monograph. Unlike the owner of an existing building, the newly constructed building must rent all the space at the current market rent. When rents are declining, the new building has no protection from these declines. Thus, the financial situation would deteriorate much more than indicated in figure 1.9, where existing leases, written when rents were higher, protect the landlord.

Many decisions in the office market are driven by the potential to earn profits. NOI is a good measure of operating profit (i.e., profit before considering income taxes, profit taxes, or financing expenses [e.g., interest paid]). Thus, the slow growth in NOI after 1983 has important implications for investment, development, and leading decisions. These implications are explored throughout this book, particularly in chapters 3, 6, and 7.

INTERDISCIPLINARY NATURE OF OFFICE MARKET RESEARCH

This review identifies major themes that cut across disciplines. The evaluation of alternative methods reveals a surprising amount of complementarity; that is, a substantial number of differences in methodology can be viewed as interlinking rather than as competitive. Nevertheless, much of the office market literature is in British and European journals, and there is little exchange of ideas among the disciplines or across the Atlantic.

The biologist Stephen Jay Gould (1980) has provided an argument for interdisciplinary research. After reviewing Darwin's journals and other writing, he concluded that the theory of natural selection is an extended analogy to the laissez-faire economics of Adam Smith. Darwin's discovery of natural selection did not derive exclusively from the massive data he collected during the journey of the *Beagle*. Rather, Darwin's reading outside biology (e.g., the writings of Malthus and Smith) led to his supposition that the order of nature, like the wealth of nations, derives from a struggle among individuals for their own welfare. Gould concluded that "inductivism is inadequate, that creativity demands breadth, and that analogy is a profound source of insight" (p. 68).

The value of interdisciplinary research is a major theme in this book. The benefits of integrating various segments of the office market literature are emphasized—in particular, specific suggestions for melding findings from the "European" and North American literature are made in chapters 4 and 5. This interdisciplinary concept can be applied in specific ways to the office market. For example, Fisher (1992) has stressed that office market research should integrate the capital markets (e.g., the supply of funds from large institutions to office markets) with the rental market for office space (e.g., the spatial distribution of supply and demand for space). Net rental income from office buildings becomes a cash flow to capital markets. Fisher points out that this cash flow becomes securitized by capital market investors, who are concerned only about how it affects the risks and returns of their portfolios. He suggests that the cash flows from office buildings have not been priced properly relative to cash flows from other assets.

Capital markets are overlooking the important spatial dimension of the office cash flows that they buy. As argued by Pollakowski, Wachter, and Lynford (1992), it is impossible to evaluate the risks and returns associated with office cash flows without evaluating the different metropolitan markets in which offices function. Thus, the spatial dimension of office market analysis is investigated here in chapter 4.

Fisher and Webb (1992) identified a number of substantive issues for future office market research, many of these relating to use and measurement of rates of return on real estate. These issues include better measurement of effective rental rates over time, better measurement of rates of return including capital appreciation in real estate values, better identification of macroeconomic factors influencing rates of return, and better measures of the benefits of diversifying into ownership of office buildings and other real estate assets.

OVERVIEW OF REMAINDER OF VOLUME

This final section provides a brief review of the remainder of the monograph.

Chapter 2 develops a framework for understanding the office market and office cycles. It begins with equilibrium in the office markets—that is, a situation whereby tenants, builders, and investors are satisfied with rental rates, vacancies, and the supply of space. Forces that cause the office market to change are then examined. The concept of the natural or normal vacancy rate is the most important idea to emerge in this chapter. Landlords want to hold a certain amount of vacant space so that they can repair the property and search for the best tenants. The amount of vacant space that they want to hold, divided by the total amount of space, is the natural vacancy rate. It is an equilibrium rate because there is no reason for landlords to alter the natural vacancy rate.

Chapter 3 explores two methods for measuring the natural vacancy rate. Most models designed to forecast the office market use the natural vacancy rate concept. They also account for changes in demand, changes in construction costs, and other variables that influence office cycles. Chapter 3 begins by discussing research that examines these issues. It then evaluates sophisticated econometric models geared to explaining historical office market cycles.

Chapters 4 and 5 discuss research themes common to several branches of the literature, including: the spatial implications of face-to-face contacts among office employees; the trend toward suburbanization and regional deconcentration of office employment; and forecasts of future growth in office space and employees. The contribution of each branch of the literature to each theme is evaluated and compared. Chapter 5 focuses on public policy aspects of office markets. It develops the way in which office employment is a "basic" cause of growth and decline in local and regional economies.

Chapter 6 reviews applications of the tools developed in earlier chapters. It starts with two forecasting models. The first model has a simple structure in which a forecast of employment growth drives forecasts of the office market. The second model elaborates this cause by considering forecasts for the growth in employment by occupation (e.g., managerial, technical, professional, and clerical). Rosen's essay at the end of this monograph provides a sophisticated example of these concepts.

Forecasts on office space, rental rates, expenses, and vacancies require estimates of the growth of office supply. Chapter 6 explores simple ways to use information on new construction and building permits to forecast office supply. It looks at ways to analyze trends in rents and expenses, and evaluates the repetitive up-and-down cycles that are typical of vacancy rates, rents, and new construction.

No one can forecast the office market with a high degree of certainty. Nevertheless, forecasts are useful for establishing a range of likely outcomes. Chapters 6 and 7 explore risk analysis by developing ways to examine alternative outcomes; a good office market forecast looks at a range of possible outcomes, not a single forecast. (Rosen's essay at the end of this monograph illustrates this idea.)

Chapter 7 applies the instruments of office market analysis to a case example, a specific office project. It discusses the implications of alternative assumptions about the office market for cash flow, borrowing needs, net operating income, and net present value for a proposed office building, thus showing how a study of the office market can be used to evaluate market and financial risks.

The final two essays in this volume, by Raper and Ihlanfeldt, and Rosen, respectively, elaborate upon themes addressed in the earlier chapters. Raper and Ihlanfeldt, building upon their 1990 study, investigate the ways in which office-location decisions differ among users. They discuss factors related to type of industry, organizational structure, size, age, and optimizing behavior of different office users. In the process, they emphasize one of the central themes of this monograph—that institutional detail is crucial in office-location decisions.

Rosen, using the Birch (1986) approach described in chapter 6, forecasts the demand for office space in the U.S. market to the year 2000. After analyzing sectors of office employment, he forecasts the employment in those sectors to obtain a forecast of office employment. He then analyzes the space intensity of employment. By combining the latter two forecasts—office employment and space intensity—he thus generates a demand forecast.

Notes

1. Throughout this monograph the terms *office activities* and *office markets* are used to refer collectively to office employment, space, and vacancy and rental rates.

2. Good long-term data are available on only one aspect of this structural shift: changes in employment by industry.

3. Office space per worker grew over this period and has a continued a general upward trend since (see Rosen's commentary at the end of this volume for more details). This is partly the result of the increasing use of computers, which also absorb office space.

4. Charles River Associates (1981, appendix A) provided a detailed breakdown of office occupations. Their study included managerial, technical, professional, and clerical workers, some sales workers, college and university occupations, and health work-

ers, and discussed some of the issues relevant to the choice of office occupations. Louargand (1981) discussed conceptual approaches to defining office activities.

5. The "actors" or participants in the office market are indicated in figure 1.7 by shaded rectangles, whereas real property, institutions, and their processes are indicated by clear rectangles.

6. Benjamin, Sa-Aadu, and Shilling's (1992) sample of 206 leases from Greensboro, N.C., included 87 (42 percent) with relocation provisions.

7. Rental rates are typically higher when these options are included in the lease. Also, the space that a tenant is allowed to relinquish under the contraction option may not be the best; the rents (per square foot) saved on relinquished space may be less than the rent on space retained.

8. Tenant improvements are also referred to as "fitup costs."

9. This concept is particularly useful to Wheaton and Torto (1992) because the dollar amounts are available to them from a database maintained by Coldwell Banker.

10. They did not find statistical significance for variables such as CPI escalation, free parking spaces, or building quality. But improved econometric techniques (allowing interaction between base rent and lease terms) may produce better results in the future.

11. These data are obtained by the Building Owners and Managers Association (BOMA) from its members. Members represent the largest and oldest buildings, so the data do not represent all buildings. Also, the data presented are for buildings in the United States.

Chapter Two

OFFICE MARKET CYCLES: THE NATURAL VACANCY RATE

This chapter presents a conceptual framework for evaluating cycles in office market employment, construction, vacancy, and rent. First, it establishes the basic concept of long-run equilibrium in the office market; that is, it explores the conditions that are required for demand and supply to be in balance. The natural vacancy rate concept is developed as part of this equilibrium analysis. The chapter then examines what happens when some change disturbs this equilibrium. This theoretical framework is useful for analyzing and forecasting short- and long-run changes in an office market. Specifically, literature on the pronounced boom-and-bust cycle in office markets is reviewed in this and the following chapter.

A substantial part of the significance of office market research derives from the cyclical behavior of the market. The depressed part of these cycles is costly in terms of profits, lost jobs, and bank failures, as well as in the waste associated with buildings that stand vacant and idle for long stretches of time. Research on office market cycles is important because it may eventually change public and private decision making. One hopes that local zoning authorities, lenders, real estate appraisers, and developers will learn to be more cautious during the boom part of the office market cycle. As knowledge of office market cycles improves, these cycles should be more easily forecastable. Thus, decision makers can use improved forecasts to avoid the worst of the negative part of office market cycles.

The concept of the natural vacancy rate (V_N) is the most important development in the office market literature in the last 15 years. The natural rate is the rate of vacancies that leaves landlords with no desire for change (i.e., landlords want to hold a certain amount of vacant space). Because of the slow response of supply to changes in demand, the actual vacancy rate (V_A) can differ substantially from the natural rate (i.e., there can be a vacancy gap, V_G, equal to the actual vacancy rate minus the natural rate [$V_G = V_A - V_N$]). When this happens, the office market is out of equilibrium and it will tend to approach the natural vacancy rate. Because both rents and construction adjust to eliminate the vacancy gap, changes in the office market are somewhat predictable.

EQUILIBRIUM IN THE OFFICE MARKET

Figure 2.1 gives a systemwide view of demand and supply in the office market. All of the values of the axes of the figure are equilibrium values: that is, none of the actors in the system (e.g., landlords, investors, developers, and tenants) has an incentive to change his or her behavior. The system should remain in equilibrium until some shock occurs (such as an unanticipated increase in demand caused by growth of office employment). The purpose of figure 2.1's diagram is to show the relationships among current demand for rental space, the asset price of real property, and supply of new construction.

Starting at the point in figure 2.1 where the dashed line meets the demand curve (upper right, quadrant I), one sees that this gives R (gross rental payments per square foot [psf]), net operating income per square foot (NOI psf), and the associated equilibrium stock of office space. For a given stock of space equal to S_1, the rental price is found on the demand curve. Gross rental rates per square foot are multiplied by one minus the operating expense ratio $(1 - OER)$ to get NOI psf, plotted on the vertical axis.

In quadrant II of figure 2.1, NOI psf is divided by the user cost of capital to obtain the asset price or value of an additional square foot of office space. If taxes are ignored, the user cost is an interest rate equal to the cost of raising debt and equity money (usually a weighted average of the two) minus the rate of increase in value. This is the cost of providing a dollar of capital to the office market.

Moving to quadrant IV of figure 2.1, the equilibrium stock of office space is associated with a certain amount of replacement construction. That is, the wearing out or abandonment of older, lower-quality office space results in construction to replace or rehabilitate this space and maintain the equilibrium office stock. It should be emphasized that C, plotted on the lower vertical axis of figure 2.1, is an equilibrium level of construction that does not cause any growth or decline in the amount of office space. The amount of this construction

Figure 2.1 EQUILIBRIUM DEMAND AND SUPPLY FOR OFFICE SPACE

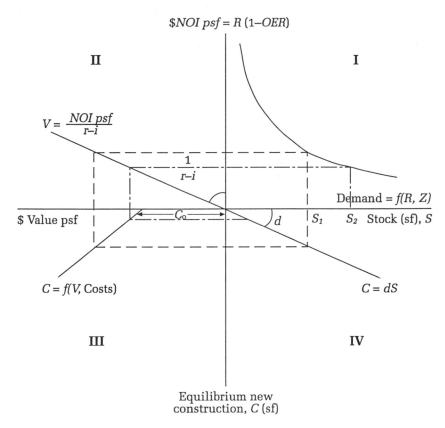

$NOI psf = R (1–OER)$

II

I

$V = \dfrac{NOI\ psf}{r-i}$

$\dfrac{1}{r-i}$

Demand $= f(R,\ Z)$

$ Value psf

C_0

d

S_1 S_2 Stock (sf), S

$C = f(V,\ \text{Costs})$

$C = dS$

III

IV

Equilibrium new
construction, C (sf)

Source: Adapted from Wheaton and DiPasquale (forthcoming).
Notes: R, gross rent per square foot (psf); OER, total operating expenses and vacancy losses as a ratio to gross rent; NOI psf = R(1−OER) = net operating income per square foot; r, the discount rate; i, expected inflation in value; V, value psf; C, new construction (sf); d, depreciation rate of the stock; Z, other economic variables such as real gross national product (GNP) and office employment. The functional form, f(V, Costs), specifies that construction goes up as value increases and decreases as costs rise.

depends on the rate of physical depreciation and obsolescence of existing space.

Quadrant III, in the lower left of figure 2.1, gives the marginal cost of building new office space to replace the space that has worn out. This is a standard supply schedule from economics. It shows the cost of commanding the resources (labor, material, and capital equipment) to build an extra square foot of space. The more space that must be built, the higher the cost of coaxing these resources away from other sectors of the economy. In equilibrium, this supply schedule depends only on replacement cost (i.e., the cost to replace worn-out space), not on expectations about the value of space. C_0 is the minimum cost of replacing space and marginal cost rises for additional construction.

To complete the dashed line in figure 2.1, it is necessary to draw a vertical line from the replacement cost schedule to the value schedule in the quadrant II. The office market is in equilibrium only if this vertical line intersects with the horizontal line from the demand side. For example, if one had started with a higher stock of space, S_2, then equilibrium rents and value would be so low that most new construction would be choked off (see the dot-dash line, figure 2.1).[1] With insufficient construction to replace the stock of space that wears out or becomes obsolete, the stock will decline until it reaches the equilibrium level, S_1.

COMPARING ALTERNATIVE EQUILIBRIA

Suppose the equilibrium in figure 2.1 is shocked by an increase in demand (see figure 2.2). Because it takes a long time to plan and build new office space, there will be no immediate change in supply.[2] Rents and NOI on existing buildings will rise by the amount labeled *IR* in figure 2.2. Given rising rents due to greater demand for an existing amount of space, vacancy rates will tend to fall. The rise in rents and decline in vacancy rates will encourage developers and investors to build more space. Eventually, the stock of space will rise to S_2, an amount consistent with the new, higher, demand.

Figures 2.1 and 2.2 are not well suited to analyzing dynamic changes because one cannot see how vacancy rates, rental rates, and construction move during the adjustment toward a new equilibrium.[3] For example, one can see replacement construction in figure 2.2 (quadrant IV), but not that the amount of new space built must rise above replacement construction to move the stock of existing space from S_1 to S_2. I turn, therefore, to another diagram suitable for analyzing dynamic movements from one equilibrium to the next.

Figure 2.2 A SHOCK TO DEMAND (*D'*), CAUSING SUPPLY VALUE AND
CONSTRUCTION TO ADJUST TO HIGHER EQUILIBRIUM LEVELS

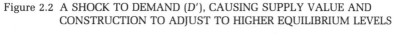

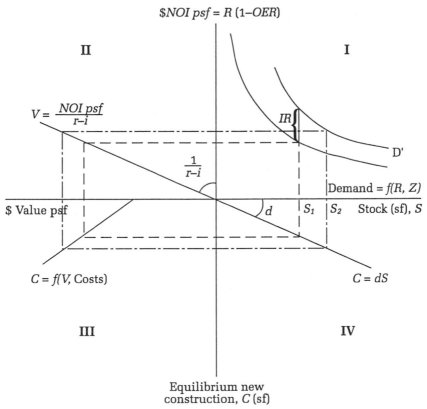

$NOI\ psf = R\ (1-OER)$

II   I

$V = \dfrac{NOI\ psf}{r-i}$ IR

$\dfrac{1}{r-i}$ D'

Demand = $f(R, Z)$

$ Value psf d S_1 S_2 Stock (sf), S

$C = f(V, \text{Costs})$ $C = dS$

III   IV

Equilibrium new
construction, C (sf)

Source: Adapted from Wheaton and DiPasquale (forthcoming).
Notes: *D'*, higher level of demand due to growth in office employment; *IR*, initial
response of rents, *R*, and *NOI psf*.

NATURAL VACANCY RATE AND LONG-RUN EQUILIBRIUM

Landlords want or need to hold some vacant space (i.e., they are
willing to rent this space only under certain conditions that are not
currently met). The natural vacancy rate is the amount of this desired
vacant space divided by the total amount of office space in the market.
The natural vacancy rate is a long-run equilibrium or optimal rate
because landlords are happy with this amount of vacant space under
the given (i.e., current) conditions.

Vacant space is like an inventory of goods held by a merchant. Landlords hold vacant space so that they can quickly satisfy the needs of those seeking to rent space. It is optimal for landlords to hold a certain amount of vacant space for the same reasons that it is optimal for a merchant to hold an inventory of the goods they sell.

To gain further perspective on the natural vacancy rate, suppose that landlords decided they didn't want any vacant space; that is, suppose all landlords reduced their rents until all the space was fully occupied. With zero vacancy, additional tenants would not be able to find available space to satisfy their needs. This would be equilvalent to finding all the shelves bare in a local store. Tenants in need of additional space would have to arrange to have it built by contracting with developers. This long and costly process would seem undesirable to tenants who know little about real estate. That is why tenants pay extra amounts of money (e.g., developers' profits) to developers and investors who build and hold vacant space.[4]

Landlords need to hold some vacant space to prepare it for rental to tenants. Part of this "frictional" vacancy is the need to search for tenants who can be relied upon to pay rent. Thus, landlords may search for tenants who are able to pay the desired rent, rather than immediately entering into a lease with the first prospective tenant. The greater the expected growth in demand, the more optimistic are landlords, so they will hold more vacant space as they search for good tenants who can pay high rents.

Of course, it is expensive for landlords to keep space vacant. They must continue to pay property taxes, insurance, interest on their mortgage, and other expenses even though no rental income is received on the space. Thus, landlords must balance the cost of holding vacant space against the benefits just discussed. Individual landlords may have different costs (e.g., different assessed values or different mortgage interest rates), so each individual may have his or her own natural vacancy rate.

The actual vacancy rate differs from the natural vacancy rate when landlords are unhappy with the amount of vacant space they hold. If they think that the amount of vacancy is too low, they will drive a hard bargain with tenants and wait to find the best possible tenant. On the other hand, if they think that the level of vacancy is too high, they will be eager to rent space to the first qualified tenant.

IMPLICATIONS OF NATURAL VACANCY RATE

The most important insight from the natural vacancy rate concept is that the change in rents depends, in large part, on the relationship between the actual vacancy rate and the natural vacancy rate (i.e., on the "vacancy gap," which equals the natural vacancy rate minus the actual vacancy rate). If the actual vacancy rate is above the natural vacancy rate, landlords will feel that vacancies are too high. They will be eager to rent space, exerting downward pressure on rents. But, if the actual vacancy rate is below the natural vacancy rate, landlords will feel they can afford to wait for better tenants and those who can pay higher rents; this will exert upward pressure on rents.

A key part of this argument is that rents are slow to adjust to changes in market conditions. There is sluggishness in the system so that vacancy rates adjust before rents adjust. There are several reasons why rents are slower to adjust than vacancies. One reason is long-term leases (typically, 3 to 15 years in the office market), which cause both landlords and tenants to be less influenced by current market conditions. Another reason is high transaction and search costs, which make it difficult to determine what the market-clearing rent should be. A final reason is that the supply of office space is slow to respond to changes in market conditions; typically, additions to the stock of office space are no more than 1 percent or 2 percent per year. Thus, it is easy to change the amount of vacant space but difficult to change the total amount of space.

This last point is a great help in modeling the office market because the supply of space can be taken as roughly fixed or highly predictable at any specific time. Thus, the vacancy rate should be the first variable to respond to changes in the demand for space. Then rents will change depending on the relationship between actual vacancy and natural vacancy and other variables (e.g., expectations of inflation). In summary, the variables that influence the natural vacancy rate include change in demand (ΔD), taxes—including the property tax (T_P) and income taxes (T_I)—insurance (I), interest rates (r), and inflation (i). The functional relationship for the natural vacancy rate is as follows:

$$V_N = f(\Delta D, T_P, T_I, I, r, i). \qquad (2.1)$$

Here, the symbol $f(\ )$ stands for some functional relationship that will be explained next.

The natural vacancy rate increases when demand grows more rapidly because landlords can reasonably expect to charge more rent by waiting to rent their space. An increase in the income tax rate is likely to have a positive influence on the natural vacancy rate because it makes the tax shelter aspect of office investment more attractive. The cost of holding vacant space is increased by an increase in the interest rates or an increase in property taxes or insurance. This lowers the natural vacancy rate. Finally, an increase in inflation causes an increase in rents that can be expected from office space, so that the natural vacancy rate will increase.[5]

The theory can be further summarized in equation form by defining the vacancy gap:

$$V_G = V_N - V_A. \tag{2.2}$$

Changes in rental rates, ΔR, are a function of inflation and the vacancy gap:

$$\Delta R = f(i, V_G). \tag{2.3}$$

Note that the three equations that defined the most important elements of the model are interdependent. That is, variables on the left-hand side of one equation enter into the right-hand side (i.e., the explanatory variables) for another equation. The last part of this chapter discusses research designed to capture these interdependencies.

NATURAL VACANCY RATE AND OFFICE MARKET CYCLES

Figure 2.3 presents an overview of the dynamic interaction between supply and demand in the short run, and also clarifies the role of vacant space in the adjustment process. To understand the figure, begin with the natural vacancy rate, V_N. Landlords want to hold the amount of vacant space associated with V_N; this amount of space allows them to do repairs and to search for desirable tenants.[6] The natural vacancy rate in figure 2.3 is the equilibrium (or desired) amount of vacant space divided by S_1 from figure 2.1.

At the natural vacancy rate, real rents show no tendency for change. This is one of the equilibrium characteristics of V_N. In addition, construction is equal to dS (where $S = S_1$ in this case), the amount of construction just necessary to replace worn-out or obsolete office space. Thus, figure 2.3 begins with the initial equilibrium in figure 2.2: S_1 and the associated unchanging level of rent and the replacement level of construction.

To investigate dynamics, consider the unanticipated increase in demand indicated by IR in figure 2.2. More demand for the existing stock of space will cause vacancy rates to decline to $V_A{}^1$ (figure 2.3). This opens up a negative vacancy gap, V_G ; tenants eager to rent space will eventually bid rents up as indicated by the causal relationship

Figure 2.3 DYNAMIC ADJUSTMENTS IN VACANCY RATES, RENTS, AND
CONSTRUCTION

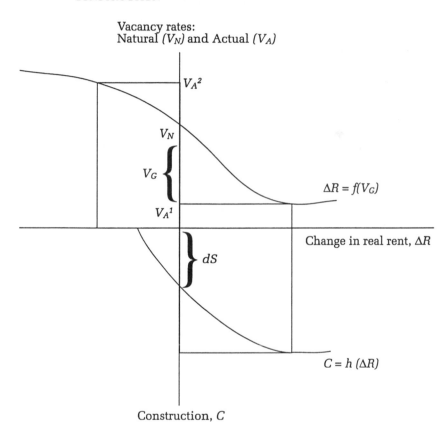

Notes: V_A^1 is the actual vacancy rate associated with the increased level of demand
indicated by IR in figure 2.2. $V_G = V_A - V_N$. V_A^2 is the actual vacancy rate associated
with overbuilding or with a reduction in demand.

between the vacancy gap and rental rates in figure 2.3. After a substantial lag, during which developers, investors, and lenders arrange to
build new space, construction increases in response to low vacancy
and high rents. Since construction rises above the replacement level,
the stock of available space eventually rises from S_1 to S_2 (figure 2.2).

From figure 2.3, it is easy to see how the office market approaches
a new equilibrium with a higher stock of space. The solid line in
the figure is associated with the initial shock to the system (IR in
figure 2.2). After this shock, construction is above the replacement

level, causing the stock of space to grow. As a consequence, the vacancy rate is increased and the vacancy gap decreases. This reduces the rate of growth of real rents. Eventually, V_A approaches V_N, the growth of rental rates stops, and new construction returns to the replacement level. But now the replacement level is associated with the new, higher stock of space, S_2.

The response of construction to a negative change in demand (e.g., a reduction in demand relative to a fixed supply) is limited. Suppose, for example, that a reduction in demand causes the actual vacancy rate to rise to $V_A{}^2$ (figure 2.3).[7] The minimum amount of construction is zero. Thus, when demand decreases, the office market may be left with high vacancy and declining rents for a considerable time period (see the dotted line in figure 2.3), while depreciation of the existing office stock and any positive growth in demand gradually bring the market back to equilibrium. This situation has existed in many local office markets since the end of the 1980s.

CRITIQUE OF NATURAL VACANCY RATE CONCEPT

The idea of the natural vacancy rate came from labor markets (an individual supplying labor might prefer to remain unemployed for a time while searching for the best job). The concept was first applied to rental housing markets by Eubank and Sirmans (1979) and by Rosen and Smith (1983). Thus, the concept is well grounded in the economics literature.

Wheaton and Torto (1992) have criticized several articles dealing with equation (2.3) on the grounds that the authors view that equation in isolation rather than as part of a simultaneous equation system. If one looks just at equation (2.3), it implies that rental rates will fall indefinitely in response to a given gap between actual and natural vacancy rates. If the change in rental rates on the left-hand side of equation (2.3) is not stated in percentage form, then it is possible for a given vacancy gap to be associated with negative *levels* of rents. Although some empirical papers have indeed estimated equation (2.3) in isolation, almost all authors have recognized that this equation is embedded in a larger dynamic system. This point was emphasized by the preceding discussion (see figures 2.1–2.3). Thus, the strongest form of the Wheaton-Torto critique (that equation [2.3] lacks any theoretical foundation) is incorrect.

Search Theory Model of Wheaton (1990) and Wheaton and Torto (1992)

An alternative to the natural vacancy rate concept has recently been developed by Wheaton (1990) and by Wheaton and Torto (1992). On this theory, rent is determined by bargaining between landlords and tenants. Landlords set the minimum rent that they will accept (their "reservation rent"), based on expected time on the market for their vacant space. The expected vacant time decreases with the flow of prospective tenants and increases with the amount of competitive space available. Similarly, the maximum rent that tenants are willing to pay for a given amount of vacant space depends on the opportunities they have available to rent other space and on the competition they perceive from other prospective tenants.

The level of rent actually paid in a given transaction is somewhere between the maximum that the tenant will pay and the minimum that the landlord will accept. Therefore, this negotiated rent will be higher when a larger number of tenants are searching for a given amount of space. The gross amount of space leased during a recent period of time can measure the flow of tenants searching for space. Likewise, the negotiated rent will be lower as the vacancy rate increases, because vacant space represents competition for landlords and opportunities for tenants. Thus, the search model suggests the following form for the optimal level of rents, R^*:

$$R^* = \beta_0 - \beta_1 V_{t-1} + \beta_2 \, Abs_{t-1}, \qquad (2.4)$$

where Abs_{t-1} is the gross absorption of space (approximately the total amount of new space leased) during the previous time period.

It may take time for the actual level of rents to adjust to the optimal level, because landlords and tenants may be slow to perceive the flow of perspective tenants or the amount of competitive space on the market. Thus, Wheaton and Torto (1992) have proposed a rent adjustment equation:

$$R_t - R_{t-1} = \mu(R^*_t - R_{t-1}). \qquad (2.5)$$

The solution to equations (2.4) and (2.5) simply says that the change in rents, ΔR_t, is a function of lagged vacancy, lagged absorption, and the level of rents lagged:

$$\Delta R_t = \mu\beta_0 - \mu\beta_1 V_{t-1} + \mu\beta_2 Abs_{t-1} - \mu R_{t-1}. \qquad (2.6)$$

An anonymous author (1992) combines search theory with the theory of the natural vacancy rate. His theory begins with office firms searching for space because they are newly formed, expanding, or relocating. The type of office space demanded by these firms depends on their characteristics: e.g., they need new suburban space or they need class B space in the central city. Some of these firms will be mismatched in the sense that they will be unable to find the type of space they need at rents they can afford. Mismatched firms will drop out of the market. The square footage of office space demanded by the remaining firms constitutes effective demand.

On the supply side, landlords are willing to rent space at the going market rate; by way of contrast, the natural vacancy rate theory says that landlords may wait for higher rents in the future. The only reasons that landlords hold vacant space is that they have been unable to find a tenant at the market rental rate. Each landlord may have his or her own idea of what the market rental rate is; landlords search for information about rents, vacancies, and the demand for space. Similarly, landlords have an expected duration of vacancy which depends on their perception about demand (measured by growth in employment or recent absorption rates) and supply (measured by the vacancy rate, changes in the vacancy rate, and recent completions). When landlords perceive that demand is high relative to supply they will raise rents and be more willing to wait to rent space. These factors contribute to a high natural vacancy rate. Conversely, when landlords perceive that there are few tenants looking for space and that there is a large amount of available space, they will lower rents and they will become eager to negotiate terms that will result in a short duration of vacancy. Therefore, the natural vacancy rate will decline.

The natural vacancy rate is the equilibrium rate in the market: the rate where effective demand is equal to effective supply.

The implications of search theory for the natural vacancy rate are not obviously different than the implications of inventory theory or labor market theory. In both cases, high employment growth leads to an increase in the natural vacancy rate. However, search theory puts less emphasis on inventory carrying costs and more emphasis on completions of new space and changes in vacancy rates as determinants of search behavior.

Critique of Search Theory Model

The search theory of Wheaton and Torto (1992) puts all of the burden for market adjustment on rents. That is, the only tool available to landlords and tenants when the market is out of equilibrium is presumed to be adjustments in the level of rents. However, many observers have been persuaded that office rental rates are slow to adjust (see, for example, Downs 1986). Furthermore, the "inventory" theory underlying the natural vacancy rate indicates that landlords should adjust vacancy rates as well as rents. Thus, the search theory model does not appear to tell the entire story about office market adjustments.

From the landlord's point of view, rents and vacancies can both be adjusted when the market is out of equilibrium. Landlords may perceive that demand is elastic, so that small adjustments in rents cause big adjustments in vacancies in the same direction.[8] Thus, landlords may focus on adjustments of the vacancy gap rather than on large adjustments in rental rates.

A more general model would allow rents to be influenced by both the natural vacancy rate and the optimal rental rate. Such a model would consist of equation (2.1), equation (2.4), and the following equation:

$$\Delta R_t = \mu(R^* - R_{t-1}) + \beta(V_N - V_{t-1}) \qquad (2.7)$$

Thus, the adjustment of rental rates could be influenced by both the natural vacancy rate and the optimal level of rents.[9]

The proposed model is not complete, because it incorporates no way for new construction to respond to rental rates and vacancy rates. Simultaneous equation models that allow for construction to respond to market conditions are discussed in chapter 3. The frontier of office market research appears to be the development of methods for combining equations (2.2), (2.4), and (2.7), along with the other equations required by the supply side. The development of appropriate data (e.g., on effective rental rates) and estimation techniques will undoubtedly be part of this new frontier.

CONCLUSIONS AND DIRECTIONS FOR FUTURE RESEARCH

This chapter has summarized the theory behind office market dynamics. It has reviewed the basic causes of changes in office demand, supply, and market conditions (i.e., lease term, vacancy rate, and rental rate). The theory begins with an equilibrium in office markets where landlords, tenants, developers, lenders, and related professionals are earning normal returns for their efforts. It proceeds to show what happens when the equilibrium is "shocked" by a change in demand or supply.

The most important recent concept to emerge in office market research has been the notion of the natural or normal vacancy rate and the vacancy gap, indicating disequilibrium in the market. In theory, the office market generally moves toward the natural or normal vacancy rate. For example, a positive vacancy gap (actual vacancy greater than normal vacancy) tends to be reduced as the market adjusts toward the equilibrium. Landlords will be eager to rent space, causing a decline in rental rates. Construction will also decline, in some cases to a minimum level of zero. These adjustments will stimulate demand and reduce supply as the existing stock of space gradually wears out. Thus, vacancy rates will tend to decline as the market adjusts back toward the natural vacancy rate. A similar story can be told when demand increases, causing the vacancy rate to fall below the natural vacancy rate and stimulating the construction of new space.

The theory of the natural vacancy rate explains the behavior of office market cycles as a result of unanticipated changes in supply or demand. For example, if demand unexpectedly increases, then vacancy rates will fall and rents will eventually increase. This will signal the need to build additional office space beyond the amount required to replace space that is wearing out. Since it takes a long time for new space to be planned and developed, the unanticipated increase in demand could generate a substantial cycle in vacancy rates, rents, and construction. That is, vacancy rates would go far below normal, and rents far above normal, and a substantial boom in construction would be required.

Office market theory is typically developed under the assumption that cycles are led by changes in demand. However, cycles can also be generated by changes in supply. For example, suppose that the cost of financing new office construction were to decrease unexpectedly. With no change in rents or vacancies, developers would now be interested in building additional office space. A construction boom would follow until the amount of space had increased, vacancy rates had increased, and rents had fallen to a level that provided normal profits for development and investment of office space. This supply-led theory has recently become important as an explanation of office market cycles. The evidence used to determine whether a given office market cycle is supply-led or demand-led is evaluated in chapter 3.

Recently, Wheaton and Torto (1992) have developed an alternative to the natural vacancy rate concept. Their theory is based on the idea that office rents are set by bargaining between landlords and tenants. The greater the number of tenants searching for office space, the higher the optimal rental rate set by landlords. On the other hand, a large amount of vacant space provides competition to landlords and opportunities to tenants, so the optimal rental rate declines. In Wheaton and Torto's model, actual rental rates are adjusted toward the optimal rate.

A frontier in office market research appears to involve development of a model for combining the natural vacancy rate and optimal rental rate theories. There is a need for a general framework incorporating each theory as a special case. Tests of the general model will then allow one to evaluate the relative merits of each case.

Notes

1. One can think of S_2 as being associated with a high level of vacancy; this forces rent and value down to the levels indicated by the dot-dash line in figure 2.2.

2. This assumes that the increase in demand was not anticipated by investors and developers.

3. The term *dynamics* is used to refer to the response of prices and quantities to shocks that change the long-run equilibrium of the market. In equilibrium there is no tendency to change, whereas dynamics deal with adjustments that move the market from one equilibrium to another.

4. In terms of financial markets, landlords who hold vacant space are creating a "spot" market, that is, a market for renters who need quick occupancy of space.

5. It is now fashionable to argue that real estate is not a good hedge against inflation. However, this argument seems to be based on a single historical episode (the latter part of the 1980s) when other factors caused real estate to decline at the same time that positive inflation was experienced.

6. The concept of the natural vacancy rate is investigated in more detail later in this chapter.

7. V_A^2 could be caused by high construction (overbuilding) relative to fixed or slowly growing demand. The consequences of this situation would be the same as those described in this paragraph.

8. This would occur in a model of monopolistic competition.

9. Note that inflation is captured by the R_{t-1} term in equation (2.7).

Chapter Three

EMPIRICAL RESEARCH ON OFFICE MARKET DYNAMICS

The theoretical framework discussed in chapter 2 covers general relationships among different parts of the office market. Many details, however, must still be addressed. For example, to what extent do vacancy, construction, and rents respond to given changes in taxes and interest rates? And what lags are involved in these responses?

This chapter reports on empirical research designed to test theory and to provide some of these missing details. It begins by discussing exploratory research whose purpose has been to discover relationships not obvious from the theory (e.g., how fast does new office construction respond to changes in demand?). The second part of the chapter examines empirical work designed to test for the existence of and measure the natural vacancy rate; the models are implemented using data for the United States as a whole.

The final part of the chapter summarizes empirical work aimed at testing and measuring the main components of office market dynamics (i.e., empirical models that implement the framework reported in chapter 2, figure 2.3). These empirical models are called "simultaneous-equations systems" (see figures 2.2 and 2.3). The demand increase causes vacancy rates to decrease and rental rates to increase (represented by the first equation) and, after a lag, new construction responds, causing vacancy rates to increase and rental rates to decrease (represented by the second equation). These two equations interact until a new equilibrium is reached at S_2.[1]

The national office market is a composite of all metropolitan areas where the supply and demand for office space can interact as indicated by theory. The literature indicates that it is generally best to analyze local (metropolitan area) markets (see Hekman 1985, and Clapp, Pollakowski, and Lynford 1992); nevertheless, the mobility of office tenants and spatial shifts in new office construction tie local markets together. Thus, certain broad generalities are available from the analysis of the national office market.

Table 3.1 STYLIZED FACTS ABOUT OFFICE MARKET DYNAMICS

The Demand Side

Finance, insurance, and real estate (FIRE), and services are the key office-using industries.

Employment in office-using industries has grown faster than most other employment categories, at least since World War II.

Growth in employment in office-using industries is somewhat predictable.

Change in office employment growth is a causal factor, often leading cycles in office markets.

The Supply Side

Because of long planning and construction lags, the supply of office space is fixed or highly predictable in the short run.

Supply responds with a long lag to changes in demand, vacancy, and rent.

This lagged response in supply is a major cause of office market cycles.

Since the minimum amount of construction is zero, it takes a long time for supply to respond to decreases in demand.

Lenders have provided too much capital to real estate because of deregulation and the opportunity to earn large fees for loan origination. In addition, government insurance of deposits has encouraged lenders to extend risky real estate loans.

Market Conditions

The length of office leases is typically 3 to 15 years.

Office lease length has tended to shorten, with 3- to 5-year leases much more common than they were 15 years ago.

Vacancy rates respond to changes in demand before rental rates respond.

The natural or normal vacancy rate is the equilibrium rate.

Office vacancy rates tend to return to the natural rate.

Table 3.1 summarizes some of the stylized facts about office market dynamics and the natural vacancy rate. Some explanations for these facts are presented in this chapter along with possible areas for additional research. These facts appear to apply broadly to office markets in most metropolitan areas.

EXPLORATORY EMPIRICAL WORK ON OFFICE DYNAMICS

National Office Markets

Barth and colleagues (1988) analyzed the relationship between real estate cycles and cycles in the general level of U.S. economic activity.

Nonresidential U.S. construction activity, the authors' closest approximation to office markets, is less closely related to business cycles than housing construction. But the authors found systematic relationships that suggest the possibility of forecasting cycles in office construction with a reasonable degree of accuracy.

Downs (1986) pointed out that office rents and estimated (appraised) market values seemed to be too high in 1986, considering the high vacancy rates at that time. He suggested several institutional reasons for this, including: (1) differences between effective rents and contract rents (i.e., the result of subtracting concessions given by landlords to tenants); (2) long lease terms, causing gross rental receipts to respond slowly; (3) reluctance of financial institutions to report losses, causing high appraised values; (4) interest rate reductions, causing the present value of income to rise; and (5) federal tax law that encouraged investment in real estate.

Kling and McCue (1987) used a simultaneous-equation model, with national data on the value of office construction as a dependent variable, to test some of these hypotheses.[2] They found that interest rates, interacting with the level of output in the economy, are the most important determinants of national office construction. They uncovered no evidence that tax law changes influenced office construction significantly.

Trends and Cycles in Local Office Markets

Kelly (1983) argued that the risks associated with office development could be substantially reduced by analyzing trends and cycles in local office employment. He pointed out that employment forecasts from econometric models and shifts in employment in office-using industries help to forecast the demand for office space. With knowledge of the supply side from permits, the office developer can make informed decisions about the right time to construct a new building.

Kelly (1983) reviewed annual data from New York City on the supply of new space and on vacancy rates. He stated that net absorption (net change in occupied space) can be estimated from new construction and change in vacant space. On the demand side, he used employment in white-collar occupations by industry to estimate the amount of office employment by industry. Office-using industries are those with a significant amount of white-collar (managerial, professional, technical, and clerical) employment. Similar estimates of demand have been made by Wheaton and Torto (1985) and by Birch (1986) (a detailed discussion of the Birch method is provided in chapter 6). All of these authors have used forecasts of industry employment from econometric models to derive estimates of the demand for office space.

Kroll (1984) mined secondary data sources for information relevant to causes of growth of office activities in San Francisco's suburbs. The author's information was organized according to locational factors: (1) transportation and commuting; (2) housing price and quality; (3) labor force characteristics; and (4) other characteristics such as availability of utilities. The forecasting methodology for this study was eclectic, utilizing trend analysis, a ratio method, and regression analysis.[3] Sensitivity analysis was done with high, low, and most-likely forecasts. The variety of forecasting methods reinforced the sensitivity analysis by establishing a range of plausible forecasts.

A theoretical framework constructed around supply and demand functions (see chapter 2) is implicit in Kroll's (1984) research. Her major conclusion was that supply was projected to grow much more rapidly than demand over a 10-year period, provided that then-current building plans were not modified. Kroll recognized that the interaction between supply and demand, reflected in vacancy rates and rental rates, would undoubtedly cause postponement or cancellation of some current building plans. Thus the interdependent process implied by theory was handled informally by Kroll.

Hekman (1985), recognizing that office markets are localized and therefore affected strongly by local employment growth, explored the dynamics of office markets in 14 cities over a 5-year period. In the short run (within one year), he took the supply of space as fixed. However, he assumed that vacancy rates are exogenous, an approach that conflicts with those of Rosen (1984) and Wheaton and Torto (1985). Hekman found that local office demand depends on employment, unemployment, and gross national product (GNP). He further found that long-run changes in supply (measured by the value of construction permits) was a function of growth in FIRE (finance, insurance, and real estate) employment over the 10 years previous and of current rental rates.[4]

Summary of Exploratory Empirical Work

The literature reviewed in this section has used a variety of methodologies to explore office markets. Findings suggest that changes in interest rates, employment, and production influence office markets at national and local levels. This exploratory research suggests that interest rates, employment, and production affect the demand and supply for office space. The demand change then causes alterations in vacancy rates and rental rates. These changes induce a supply response. In addition, changes in interest rates may influence supply directly by changing costs of construction.[5] Kelly (1983) and Kroll (1984) projected trends in demand and supply and then compared these projections. For example, Kroll found that supply is growing much faster than demand. As she pointed out, this means that vacancy rates will rise and rental rates will fall: that is, the office market can be expected to soften significantly in the future.

From the perspective of theory, the Kelly and Kroll exploratory research can be interpreted as attempting to forecast the dynamic pattern of a move from one equilibrium to another (e.g., the move from the equilibrium associated with one stock of space $[S_1]$ to a higher stock of space $[S_2]$; see figures 2.1–2.3). However, trend extrapolation is a simplistic way of doing this, for it does not fully capture the interactions between supply and demand. Therefore, I now turn to models that use the natural vacancy rate and to simultaneous equations systems.

ESTIMATING NATURAL VACANCY RATES

The natural vacancy rate concept has been applied to office markets by Shilling, Sirmans, and Corgel (1987), Wheaton and Torto (1992), Anonymous (1992), and Voith and Crone (1988). These authors have developed two distinct methodologies for estimating natural vacancy rates. One requires the natural vacancy rate to be constant over time and the other allows it to change over time.

Figure 3.1 illustrates two methods for finding the natural vacancy rate using data for the U.S. office market.[6] For the first method, suppose that the variables determining the natural vacancy rate are unchanging (e.g., interest rates, search costs, increases in demand, and other factors discussed in chapter 2 are all constant). Alternately, it could be assumed that the effects of these variables had been small or that they offset each other over a given time period. Then the natural vacancy rate would be unchanging; but the second approach allowing for a dynamic natural vacancy rate would be more appropriate if these variables do *not* cancel out.

The actual vacancy rates might vary from the natural vacancy rate because of random changes in demand or in the expectations of landlords (figure 3.1, panel *a*). In this situation, the natural vacancy

Figure 3.1 ALTERNATIVE METHODS FOR ESTIMATING NATURAL VACANCY
RATE

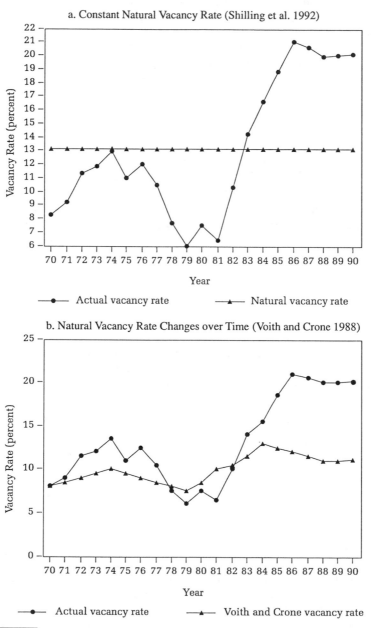

a. Constant Natural Vacancy Rate (Shilling et al. 1992)

b. Natural Vacancy Rate Changes over Time (Voith and Crone 1988)

Note: All data are for the U.S. aggregate office market.

rate would be a simple average of the actual vacancy rates, provided the average was taken over a sufficiently long time period.

Rental rates respond to the vacancy gap—the actual vacancy rate minus the natural vacancy rate. They tend to rise if the natural rate is above the actual rate and to fall if the reverse is true (see figure 2.3). A complicating factor is the effect of inflation on rental rates. If the general level of prices is rising, and especially if maintenance and operating costs for office buildings are rising, rental rates on newly leased space may increase even though the vacancy gap is positive. However, in real terms, after adjusting for the effects of inflation, rental rates generally tend to fall when the actual vacancy rate is above the natural rate.

Average rents (an average of new leases as well as leases on existing space) respond sluggishly to the difference between actual and natural vacancy rates. This is because of long lease terms and the high cost of searching for tenants who can afford to pay competitive rents. Thus, a period of six months to two years may pass before a gap between the two vacancy rates is reflected in changes in average real rent.[7]

Estimating Unchanging Natural Vacancy Rates

The model used by Rosen and Smith (1983) and by Shilling and colleagues (1987) is based on relationships among actual vacancy, natural vacancy, and rental rates. Shilling and colleagues estimated the following regression equation for 17 U.S. cities:[8]

$$\Delta R = b_0 + b_1 \Delta E - b_2 V + e, \qquad (3.1)$$

where ΔR is change in base rent per square foot, ΔE is change in operating expenses (to account for inflation), V is the actual vacancy rate, and e is a random disturbance term. They used time series for each city, 1969 through 1980, to estimate the natural vacancy rate from the constant term, b_0. Thus, this regression methodology assumes that the natural vacancy rate remains constant, just as it does in panel *a* of figure 3.1. Although this is a simplifying assumption, the regression method does allow estimation of a different natural vacancy rate for each city with sufficient data to estimate the equation.

Shilling and colleagues (1987) found natural vacancy rates ranging from 1 percent (in New York City) to over 20 percent (in Kansas City). The natural vacancy rate was relatively low in Chicago, San Francisco, and Atlanta, whereas it was relatively high in Portland, Spokane, and Pittsburgh. Although the natural vacancy rate is generally higher in more rapidly growing cities, as predicted by the theory, attempts to explain the differences among cities were only modestly successful.

There is a puzzle that demands further investigation. Estimates of the natural vacancy rate show large differences across metropolitan areas. The literature has attempted to account for these differences by examining rates of employment growth across local markets. However, it is inconsistent to argue that different rates of growth cause variations in the natural vacancy rate across metropolitan areas and at the same time to assume a constant natural vacancy rate model. It makes much more sense to view the natural vacancy rate as changing over time with local changes in the rate of growth in employment of office tenants.

Measuring Dynamic Natural Vacancy Rates

Voith and Crone (1988) developed a simple econometric model (an autoregressive process) to allow the natural vacancy rate to change over time. Using only the vacancy rate and dummy variables for time, they were able to track a natural vacancy rate that moves as in panel *b* of figure 3.1. The minimal amount of data required allowed them to estimate the model for both downtowns and suburbs for a number of metropolitan areas.

Voith and Crone (1988) generally found that office market vacancy rates are quick to adjust to the natural vacancy rate. They reported that this adjustment occurs within one or one and a half years in cities such as Boston, New York, and Hartford. However, some cities did not adjust to the natural vacancy rate during the time period covered by Voith and Crone. That is, in some cases the authors could not find the predicted relationship between natural and actual vacancy rates. This suggests that their model may be overly simplified, or that their time period was too short for accurate estimation.

Estimation of a Search Model

Anonymous (1992) has used search theory to specify a model in which the natural vacancy rate changes over time. He/she suggests that the natural vacancy rate might be a function of any one or more of the following: absorption, change in employment, construction completions, and change in the vacancy rate. It is argued that all of these variables should have a positive effect on the natural vacancy rate except completions of new office space, which should have a negative effect because an increase in supply causes landlords to reduce rent and lower the time they would like their space to be on the market. An anonymous author (1992) argues that change in the vacancy rate should be positively related to change in rent because landlords myopically extrapolate expectations. However, it seems plausible that higher vacancy rates signal softer market conditions, so the sign of the relationship with change in rents should be negative. From this point of view, his empirical results produce the incorrect sign on change in vacancy.

This author used semi-annual data from 1980–1988 on 24 metropolitan areas to find that the typical lag between the vacancy gap and a response by rents is one and a half years; shorter in Miami and Cincinnati. The magnitude of the response of rents (specifically, the percentage change in rents) for a 1% increase in the vacancy gap ranges from .24% in Phoenix to 1.3% in Atlanta. This response is low (less than .6%) in Los Angeles, San Francisco, Boston, and New York. It is higher (greater than .6%) in the major Southern cities such as Atlanta, Dallas, and Houston. The empirical results show some sharp fluctuations in the natural vacancy rate (e.g., from 11 percent to 7 percent to 12 percent over a three-year period in Chicago). This, together with some negative values for V_N, suggests that some refinement is needed in the model.

Wheaton and Torto (1992) estimated their search model (chapter 2, equation [2.6]) with data on five cities: Denver, Cincinnati, Houston, San Francisco, and Washington, D.C. The coefficients of their equation were significant with the expected signs: changes in rents were positively influenced by absorption, negatively influenced by the vacancy rate, and negatively influenced by the level of rents lagged by six months. Furthermore, they found that rents adjusted rather quickly toward their optimal level. The rate of adjustment was 50 percent or more annually, except in San Francisco, where it was about 25 percent annually. Voith and Crone (1988) also found a rapid rate of adjustment; however, their finding was for the actual vacancy rate adjusting toward the natural vacancy rate.

Wheaton and Torto (1992) have argued that the statistical significance of their model demonstrates its superiority over the natural vacancy rate concept. However, the natural vacancy rate model is not nested in the Wheaton and Torto model, so a true statistical test of one versus the other has yet to be conducted. Such a test awaits the development of a more general model that incorporates adjustment toward the natural vacancy rate and adjustment toward the optimal rental rate as special cases.

Summary of Literature on the Natural Vacancy Rate

The natural vacancy rate is a crucial variable in the theory of office market dynamics. Therefore, the measurement of the natural vacancy rate is an important part of empirical work designed to explain and predict the office market. One approach to measurement assumes that the natural vacancy rate is constant over specific periods of time. Since this requires very special assumptions about the variables that determine the natural vacancy rate (e.g., that they are constant or that they roughly cancel out over time), there has been interest in more flexible ways of measuring the natural vacancy rate. One such method (see figure 3.1, panel b) assumes a mechanical statistical process that does not allow explicitly for changes in the variables that explain the natural vacancy rate (see equation [3.1]).[9]

Shilling and colleagues (1992) have recently compared several estimates of the natural vacancy rate by metropolitan areas (table 3.2). The first column of the table is based on a constant natural vacancy rate model, whereas the other columns allow some variation over time in the natural vacancy rate. The numbers in the table are averages over the entire time period specified. There is a reasonably high correlation among these various estimates of the natural vacancy rate. The overall averages across cities are reasonably close. It is encouraging that the different methodologies produce some consistency in estimates of the natural vacancy rate.

As pointed out by Shilling and colleagues (1992), a logical next step is to model shifts in the structure of the relationships that produce the natural vacancy rate. For example, office tenants are tending to move to the suburbs, and the tenant mix is shifting toward smaller office firms. Leases are becoming shorter and tenant turnover higher. Many metropolitan areas have instituted slow-growth policies that limit office growth. The implications of these major changes in the tax law for the natural vacancy rate have not been explored.

USING VACANCY GAP TO EXPLAIN OFFICE CYCLES

Using Vacancy Gap to Forecast Rents

Wheaton and Torto (1988) used an index of office market rents for the United States to estimate rental adjustment associated with the

Table 3.2 ESTIMATES OF NATURAL VACANCY RATES IN COMMERCIAL
OFFICE BUILDINGS FOR SELECTED U.S. CITIES UNDER
ALTERNATIVE MODELS

City	1 Without Interaction Term (%)	2 With Interaction Term (%)	3 With Squared Term (%)	4 Voith and Crone's Estimates (%)	5 Anonymous' Estimates (%)
Atlanta	10.0	6.3	6.6	17.6	13.2
Baltimore	5.9	13.9	1.9	2.5	—
Chicago	8.0	4.1	5.5	7.2	8.2
Cleveland	5.7	2.8	1.4	9.9	—
Denver	20.0	12.3	4.6	14.6	8.3
Des Moines	5.1	9.9	4.1	—	—
Detroit	6.7	11.8	3.3	—	—
Indianapolis	7.6	6.5	5.4	—	—
Minneapolis	1.4	4.5	3.5	—	—
New York	—	1.0	0.2	5.8	6.1
Philadelphia	3.2	9.5	6.5	8.3	8.7
Pittsburgh	8.2	10.0	3.4	5.7	—
Portland	23.9	16.0	4.7	—	—
San Francisco	—	2.9	1.9	—	6.9
Seattle	4.9	8.4	4.0	—	—
Spokane	9.7	10.5	5.7	—	—
Mean	8.59	8.15	3.91	8.95	8.57

Notes: Models 1, 2, and 3 use data for 1960–75; Voith and Crone (1988)—model 4—
use data for 1979–87; Anonymous (1992)—model 5—used data for 1980–88. Dashes
(—) indicate data not available for those cities.
Source: Reproduced, by permission, from Shilling et al. (1992): 141. © *Journal of
Urban Economics*, 1992.

gap between actual and natural vacancy rates.[10] They found that the
natural vacancy rate trended upward during 1968 through 1986 at
the rate of about .4 percent per year. They also reported a "strong
rental adjustment mechanism" (p. 434) (that is, they found strong
confirmation of equation 2.3). In particular, they found that rents
adjust by about 2.3 percent for each 1 percent of the vacancy gap.
Glascock, Jahanian, and Sirmans (1990) indicated similar results
using building-level data for Baton Rouge.

Wheaton and Torto used data from 1973 to 1986 to forecast office
rents through 1992. They generate optimistic, pessimistic, and most-
likely scenarios depending on assumptions about the trend in the
natural vacancy rate and inflation. Thus, they demonstrate that this
type of model has potential value for forecasting.

Figure 3.2 uses actual data to illustrate complex interactions over

Figure 3.2 INTERACTIONS BETWEEN VACANCY RATES, RENTAL RATES, AND
NEW CONSTRUCTION IN U.S. OFFICE MARKET, 1970–90

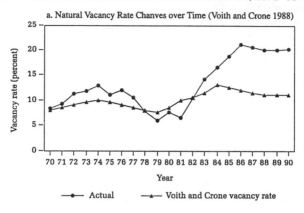

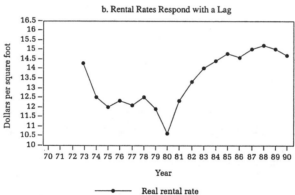

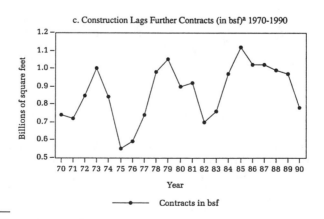

a. bsf, billions of square feet.

time in the U.S. office market. Panel *a* of figure 3.2 simply reproduces panel *b* of figure 3.1. Panel *b* of figure 3.2 depicts the average rental rate in real terms (i.e., deflated by the consumer price index) for existing as well as new leases. It is constructed from data published by the Building Owners and Managers Association (BOMA) for a constant sample of buildings.[11] Panel *c* of the figure estimates new office space constructed per year in billions of square feet (bsf).

The 1970–76 Cycle

The story told by figure 3.2 begins after 1970, when vacancy rates rose to double digits in 1972. My imperfect estimates of the natural vacancy rate show that these double-digit actual vacancy rates were substantially above the natural rate. Thus, a positive vacancy gap opened up in the early 1970s; this gap grew until 1974.

After the recession of 1969–70, the demand for office space increased for three years. But the construction boom that accompanied this recovery was more than adequate to accommodate the additional demand: office vacancy rates rose during 1971, 1972, and 1973. Many observers have attributed this to overbuilding resulting from an increase in the supply of investment capital to real estate. During this time, real estate investment trusts (REITs) were popular investment vehicles. These trusts, created by a 1960 act of Congress, gave preferred tax status to REITs in return for restrictions on the kind of investment (almost exclusively real estate) and on payments to investors (over 90 percent of earnings must be paid out to investors). Thus, REITs operated much like mutual funds, except that they specialized in ownership and/or lending related to real estate.

The notion that the popularity of REITs fueled the construction boom of the early 1970s is a departure from the theory developed in chapter 2. The popularity of REITs is not part of the strict profit-maximizing framework assumed in that chapter.[12] Instead, it represents a change in attitude toward the risks and returns associated with real estate.[13] Thus, institutional structure has been introduced as an explanation of overbuilding in office markets.

Dokko and Edelstein (1992) have developed a conceptual model in which imperfect information and transactions costs play a key role. They contend that these realities of the office market have important implications for the dynamic paths of market equilibrium prices and output, and they emphasize the need for greater institutional detail in office market research.

Real rental rates responded to the large and growing gap between actual and natural vacancy rates by declining in 1974 and 1975. Construction responded to vacancy increases after a time lag (panel *c*, figure 3.2); a large decline occurred in 1974–75, along with the decline in rental rates.

The 1976–82 Cycle

The next part of the cycle occurred as demand increased strongly after 1976, causing vacancy to fall to single digits by 1978. Vacancy bottomed out at about 6 percent in the 1979–81 period.

The response to the decline in average vacancy rates was slow and complex. It took four years for average real rents to respond by rising after 1980. Construction responded in two parts, first increasing in 1977–79. This was a very quick response, indicating that the industry was either optimistic (and, as it turned out, correctly so) or that it used forecasting techniques to anticipate the rise in demand.[14] The second part of the response, in 1982–84, was to the rise in real rental rates and possibly to changes in the tax law in 1981. This response occurred with a two-year lag.

The 1983–90 Cycle

A final cycle was associated with slow growth in demand during the period following 1983. Vacancy rates rose strongly during this period to over 20 percent. Average real rent did not respond until 1987, and then remained roughly constant for three years. Construction did not respond until 1986, a three-year lag. The ultimate response of construction, near-zero construction in many markets, did not occur until 1990, at which point vacancy rates had been greater than 20 percent for five years.

During this period, demand decreased in an important region of the country, the "oil patch." Those areas specializing in production and exploration of oil suffered from a worldwide decline in oil prices during the first part of the 1980s. This caused a regional recession that reduced the demand for office space. Even after the reductions in demand became apparent, the supply of office space continued to rise in the oil patch. Consequently, vacancy rates in these areas rose to 20 percent, and in some areas, to more than 30 percent.

A similar pattern was repeated in areas unrelated to oil production during 1988 to 1990. Demand slowed down but production remained high, causing vacancy rates to rise to the 20 percent range. This suggests that the causes of downward cycles in office markets range far beyond declines in oil prices or other declines in demand.

Institutional Explanations of Three Cycles

Several hypotheses are consistent with the dynamic pattern in figure 3.2. A widely held belief is that developers, investors, and lenders are myopic. That is, they cannot predict the future of office demand, so they respond incautiously to current market conditions.[15] Because of long lags in the planning and construction process, the office market is out of adjustment for years before supply begins to respond to changes in demand.

The institutional structure of mortgage lenders may be a cause of cycles in office markets. Important institutional characteristics include the following:

1. A very large percentage of investment in office development and ownership is financed by mortgage lenders;[16]
2. When rental rates and market prices decline, lenders bear a large part of the costs of failure. That is, lenders bear a substantial part of the risks, but they have limited potential to earn returns if the project is successful.
3. Lenders are partially protected from the risk of failure by government deposit insurance at the state and federal levels.
4. Lenders earn large fees from originating mortgage loans. This gives them the incentive to originate a large volume of loans without adequate consideration for the quality of those loans.
5. There was a substantial reduction of the regulation of lenders during the early 1980s. Reduced regulations gave lenders greater freedom to invest in risky real estate loans.

Some observers believe that lenders play the most important role in office market cycles. This view gains support from the 1983–90 cycle, when lenders appeared overly eager to extend loans up until 1989; after 1989 lenders pulled back sharply. The assumption also gains support from the 1970–75 cycle. At that time, many of the REITs were owned or controlled by commercial banks or other lenders.

An alternative hypothesis argues that tax law changes are major causes of office market dynamics. For example, tax shelters created in 1981 may have set off a building boom during the middle part of the 1980s. However, changes in tax laws enacted in 1986 eventually snuffed out the boom period. Hendershott and Kane (1992) blame the federal government for the excess supply of office space during most of the 1980s. They point out that the large depreciation allowances permitted by the 1981 Economic Recovery Tax Act imply that investors can get their money back quickly. Thus, these investors have little interest in the long-term economic viability of the project. The possibility of high vacancy rates and of declining rental rates is not of great concern to them.

Lenders, on the other hand, should have been concerned about the risk of high vacancies and low rental rates. However, Hendershott and Kane (1992) assert that the low premiums charged by the government for deposit insurance encouraged lenders to ignore these risks. Specifically they argue that lenders: required little equity from investors; underpriced their loans and equity investments; rapidly expanded their most risky investments such as nonresidential mortgages; and ignored traditional methods of risk reduction.[17] Also, Japanese investors and pension funds were expanding their investments in real estate, contributing to new construction in the face of declining growth in demand.

It would be a mistake to place too much emphasis on the role of government policy (deregulation and changes in the tax law) in office market cycles. The argument against these factors has been stated by Jeremy Siegel (1992): "These factors did not exist abroad, yet Japan and the U.K. are suffering sharp real estate downturns" (p. 5). Also, Kling and McCue (1987) found no evidence that tax law changes influence office construction.

Still another hypothesis holds that risk preferences and/or assessments of risk change over time. During building booms, lenders, investors, and developers minimize risks, emphasizing the persistent rapid growth in office demand over long time periods. But when markets are persistently overbuilt, these same actors become pessimistic. This causes office market construction to decline.

All of these hypotheses may have some degree of validity. A Salomon Brothers report by David Shulman and Sandon Goldberg (1992) summarizes many of these hypotheses. Figure 3.3, reproduced from that report, reviews a 22-year history of office demand (an estimate of U.S. office employment growth) and supply (construction of new office space). Clearly, those authors put heavy emphasis on institutional factors such as the behavior of REITs and savings and loans (S&Ls). They cite large, well-known deals by a major office developer, Olympia & York, as well as the behavior of Japanese investors.

Office Market Conditions in 1992–93

Byrne and Goldberg (1992) evaluated office markets in London and New York. They reported 40–50 percent decreases in office property

Figure 3.3 OFFICE CONSTRUCTION CONTRACTS VERSUS OFFICE EMPLOYMENT GROWTH, 1972–82

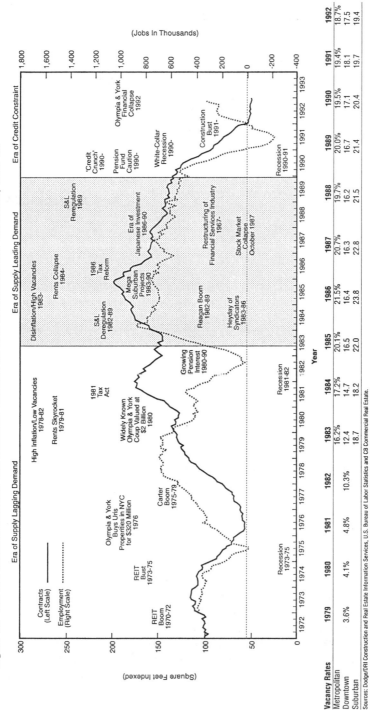

Vacancy Rates	1979	1980	1981	1982	1983	1984	1985	1986	1987	1988	1989	1990	1991	1992
Metropolitan	3.6%	4.1%	4.8%	10.3%	16.2%	17.2%	20.1%	21.5%	20.7%	19.7%	20.0%	19.5%	19.4%	18.7%
Downtown					12.4	14.7	16.5	16.4	16.3	16.2	16.7	17.1	18.1	17.5
Suburban					18.7	18.2	22.0	23.8	22.8	21.5	21.4	20.4	19.7	19.4

Sources: Dodge/DRI Construction and Real Estate Information Services, U.S. Bureau of Labor Statistics and CB Commercial Real Estate.

Source: Giliberto and Lydon 1993. Used by permission of Salomon Bros.

Notes: Square feet indexed, December 1971 = 100; 12-month moving average of contracts; 12-month change in jobs in thousands.

Figure 3.4 U.S. OFFICE MARKET CONDITIONS, JUNE 1992

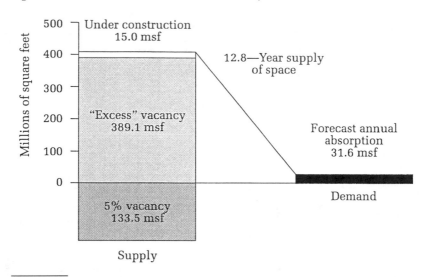

Source: Salomon Brothers, 1993, "U.S. Office Market," Jan. 5, figure 6, p. 6. Used by permission.
a. msf, millions of square feet.

values from their peaks in the late 1980s. They also found that yields on buildings that have reached stabilized occupancy ranged between 8½ percent and 13 percent in London and between 8 percent and 11 percent in New York.[18] These yields compared favorably to inflation and to short-term interest rates, whereas yields during most of the 1980s compared unfavorably.

When Byrne and Goldberg (1992) compared London and New York to smaller cities, they noted a tendency for smaller cities to quickly reach maturity and begin a declining phase. They argued that the larger cities are more likely to undergo phases of renewal and enhanced growth, and hypothesized a cyclical pattern primarily in the larger cities.

Giliberto and Lydon (1993) report that the U.S. office market has been characterized by slow or negative job growth and absorption, a situation that has driven new construction to very low levels. Thus, they find that 1992 absorption rates were well ahead of the completion of new space in all regions except the Northeast. They contend that "year supply," defined by vacant space divided by the current absorption rate, is a better indicator of market conditions than the vacancy rate alone (see figure 3.4). For example, year supply has increased dramatically since the mid-1980s, whereas the vacancy rate has remained relatively stable at a high level. Thus, year supply has tracked the deterioration in the office market over this time period, whereas the vacancy rate has not.

EVALUATING DYNAMICS WITH SIMULTANEOUS-EQUATION SYSTEMS

Rosen (1984), Wheaton and Torto (1985), and Wheaton (1987) used the natural vacancy rate concept in models designed to predict new construction, absorption, changes in vacancy, and changes in rental rates.[19] These models were developed directly out of the theory discussed earlier in this chapter. According to this theory, office market forecasts depend on accurate predictions of employment growth in office-using industries (i.e., office market dynamics are led by the demand side). Since supply is very slow to adjust, the first adjustment is in the vacancy rate; then rental rates adjust slowly; and, finally, new construction adjusts to changes in demand. These complex interactions among demand, market conditions, and supply were modeled by the preceding authors using simultaneous-equation estimation techniques.

Wheaton and Torto (1985) and Wheaton (1987) built a five-equation forecasting model with three behavioral equations and two identities. The supply-side equation relates building permits to lagged vacancy rates (the measure of market conditions) and lagged absorption rates (demand). Lags are needed because supply responds to earlier vacancy and absorption information. The second equation relates the amount of office space completed (square footage) to lagged values of office building permits. The third behavioral equation deals with demand as measured by absorption. Absorption responds to employment growth, market conditions, and an indication of recessions in the national economy. The authors argue that vacancy rates constrain absorption when the supply of available space is very limited. It is not clear from their presentation whether they include this constraint in their demand equations.

The forecasting model is completed with two identities, one of which updates the stock of office space with the amount of new completions, and the other of which estimates current vacancy rate from past vacancy rate, new construction, and office space absorption. Unlike Rosen (1984), Wheaton and Torto (1985) and Wheaton

(1987) have no prices or interest rates in their model. They state that they did not find financial variables to be statistically significant. The omission of rental rates would appear to be related to the lack of adequate data at the national level at the time their paper was written. This suggests that the vacancy rate variable is a proxy for rental rates and other market conditions. Like Rosen, Wheaton and Torto have a demand-led model that is driven by office employment forecasts.

SUMMARY AND CONCLUSIONS

Empirical research on office markets begins with exploration of relationships that appear important. This exploratory research has found that increases in interest rates cause declines in office market construction. Similarly, growth in the general level of production (e.g., change in GNP) is positively related to office construction.

A simple but often effective tool for investment and lending decisions is based on extrapolation of demand and supply. For example, change in employment by industry and occupation and changes in the square footage of office space being added to the market can be projected into the future to determine the direction of change of vacancy rates and rents. Of course, this methodology cannot capture unexpected changes in demand or supply, but it works in cases where the future growth of these variables is predicted to be similar to that in the past.

Considerable research is required on measurement of the natural vacancy rate. Three methods are currently available. One uses the relationship between rental rates and vacancy rates to estimate a natural vacancy rate for each local market area. However, this estimated natural vacancy rate is constant over time. The second method uses adjustments in vacancy rates to estimate a natural vacancy rate that is allowed to change over time in the local market. The third method is based on a search model that allows rental rates to adjust toward an optimum level with this approach; the natural vacancy rate is dynamic.

Figure 3.2 illustrates office market dynamics with actual U.S. data. It shows the strong cyclical pattern of the office market and the complex interactions, often with long lags, between vacancy rates, rental rates, and new construction. U.S. vacancy rates ranged from 6 percent to 21 percent, and real rental rates ranged from almost $15 in 1973 and again in 1986–89 to almost $11 in 1980. Finally, the construction industry is highly volatile, with new office construction ranging from .5 to 1.1 billion square feet per year.

Whereas figure 3.2 illustrates basic concepts with data for the United States as a whole, the office market works at the local level, where supply and demand interact within a given city. A great deal more research is needed on local office markets. Short time series, measurement problems, and the complexity of the market have combined to reduce the effectiveness of econometric models designed to explain local office markets.

Notes

1. More formally, a simultaneous-equation system means that two or more behavioral relationships that interact are estimated together by specialized statistical techniques.

2. Kling and McCue's (1987) estimation model is similar to one used by Barth and colleagues (1988), except that the latter used construction dollars as the dependent variable.

3. Trend analysis takes the typical historical rate of growth and projects that into the future, possibly with some modification. For example, if employment in office industries has grown 5 percent per year over some historical period (e.g., the past five years), then trend extrapolation might say that a 5 percent annual growth is expected over the next two to three years. The ratio method for forecasting uses a forecast on a large geographical area such as the nation or the state. It then uses a ratio of the local area to the broad area (e.g., office employment in the local area is 3 percent of office employment in the broad area) to adjust the forecast.

4. Hekman (1985) tried to explain cycles in office markets with a "hog market" cycle: supply responds with a lag to changes in demand, causing large swings in the market price and production. However, it is difficult to apply this model to decreases in demand, since the supply of office space (highly durable) is not easily reduced.

5. Interest expenses comprise a significant percentage (e.g., 15 percent) of construction costs.

6. The "U.S. office market" is a fiction, since office markets work at the city level. Those demanding office space need it within a particular city, and usually within a certain part of the city (e.g., downtown). The U.S. market is simply the sum of all these local markets.

7. Figure 3.2, which is discussed in more detail later in this chapter, illustrates this point.

8. Shilling et al. (1987) also experimented, unsuccessfully, with using lagged vacancy rates as explanatory variables.

9. Figure 3.1 indicates realistic orders of magnitude for natural vacancy rates in the 1970s and 1980s. Shilling et al. (1987) found considerable variation across metropolitan areas in natural vacancy rates.

10. The rental index used by Wheaton and Torto (1988) was developed by Salomon Brothers.

11. See chapter 1 for details on the BOMA data. Note that Downs (1986) argued that the market capitalizes the rents on the average lease, rather than valuing the building as though it were newly leased.

12. The flow of money into REITs might be viewed as reducing the cost of capital available to office markets. But this would not explain *why* the cost of real estate capital changed relative to other investments.

13. Note that REITs had been around for nearly 10 years before they became highly popular investment vehicles.

14. Based on direct observation of industry practices in the 1970s, the latter explanation seems improbable.

15. Frydl (1991) stated that "a too-easy credit supply in much of the 1980s was a principal factor leading to damaging imbalances in investment, manifested principally as an unprecedented overhang of commercial real estate" (p. 7). Similarly, Guttentag (1992) has argued that lenders are excessively present oriented, ignoring obvious risk factors.

16. In some cases, developers have been able to arrange for more than 100 percent financing of the project.

17. Specifically, construction lenders traditionally required "take-out commitments" to protect them from the risk that the building will be completed when market conditions are soft. These commitments became less common during the 1980s.

18. Stabilized occupancy leaves that building at the normal occupancy rate in the area (equaling one minus that equilibrium, or natural, vacancy rate). Byrne and Goldberg (1992) noted that zoning boards in the two cities are interested in keeping the cities alive. This makes planning and zoning more sensitive to arguments about positive economic effects from new office construction and less oriented toward aesthetic values.

19. Rosen (1984) estimated his model for San Francisco, whereas Wheaton and Torto (1985) and Wheaton (1987) used national data (i.e., aggregates and averages of local office markets).

Chapter Four

THE ECONOMICS OF OFFICE LOCATIONS

This chapter investigates the microfoundations of office markets. Growth or decline in occupied office space is intimately related to the location decisions of office firms. For example, a growing firm might decide to relocate from downtown to suburban office space where the rents are lower and landlords are willing to provide a more attractive package of lease terms and building characteristics. In like manner, the firm's decision about the number of new employees to hire is related to rent and other lease terms.

Some location decisions start with a broad geographical scope and then narrow the search for the best location. These decisions may begin with the choice of a continent or country, proceed to the choice of a region within the country, then to a city, and finally to the choice of a specific location.[1]

Location decisions can be separated into two parts: first, the *regional* decision, which includes the choice of a country or a metropolitan area; and, second, the *intraurban* choice between the central city and the suburbs. This chapter uses the tools of regional and urban economics to summarize these two types of location decisions.

Public policy influences office locations because offices are an important part of the economic health of a region or metropolitan area. For example, business activity and, particularly, retail activity has declined in most central business districts (CBDs) in North America over the past 25–35 years. But office employment has been a growing sector in many city centers, at least until the downturn starting in 1989–90. Many city governments depend on growth in the office sector to increase the property tax base and to keep the downtown economy healthy. Similarly, for many years, economic policy in Great Britain sought to disperse office locations from the London metropolitan region to less-affluent regions. This policy was designed to promote economic development as well as to encourage equitable job opportunities.

What tools do governments have that can influence the location of office activities? This and the following chapter review evidence that office locations are influenced by factors such as telecommunication facilities, availability of skilled labor, political factors, location of public buildings, availability of sites, adequate roads, public transportation, property taxes, and labor costs.

Investors, developers, lenders, realtors, and other private parties seek the best location for office properties. Their interest flows from the large dollar investments in office properties and the risk that high vacancy or low rents will reduce cash flows and diminish the ability to cover costs. Ultimately, these parties are concerned about possible loss of invested capital and bankruptcy. Similarly, office tenants sign leases that involve substantial amounts of money over a number of years, so they are concerned about finding the best location.

A FRAMEWORK FOR EXPLAINING OFFICE LOCATIONS

Office activities (i.e., employment using office space) produce two types of services: information and decisions. Information takes the form of data collected and compiled in various forms such as tables and charts, reports, legal briefs, and so on. Decisions influence the organization and conduct of work within a business organization or within the legal and political system. For example, a national or regional headquarters office might make a decision to reduce production workers, buy new machines, or reorganize the flow of work within a system of branch plants.

To produce these services, office activities use various inputs, or "factors of production." These include office space, labor, access to specialized information sources (e.g., a courthouse), computers, other forms of technology, and energy. The location of the office firm is an important aspect of the production decision. In effect, transportation to and from the office (by commuters as well as by those involved in business meetings) becomes an important factor of production in its own right. Relevant transportation costs include the commute by office workers and travel in order to implement decisions and disseminate information to appropriate users.

ECONOMIC THEORY AND OFFICE LOCATIONS

Economic theory can be used to discover several groups of factors that influence location decisions. According to economic theory, the major factors in office location are:

1. Agglomeration economies—access to specialized labor (e.g., specialists in accounting, finance, marketing, law, etc.) and to specialized facilities such as a stock exchange, a court of law, or a government office;
2. Factor costs such as rent, labor costs, and taxes;
3. Transportation costs of inputs and outputs, including commuting costs and the costs of conveying information and decisions to the final users;
4. Political factors, including government stability and exchange rates;
5. Amenities that influence the quality of life for top executives and others involved in the location decision.

These five variables correspond closely to those considered by a large literature on the location of manufacturing firms.[2] Some manufacturing firms are deemed to be heavily influenced by production costs—costs that correspond roughly to agglomeration economies and factor costs. Other manufacturing firms are deemed to be oriented toward transportation costs (item 3 in the preceding list). Finally, there are "footloose" manufacturing firms that are relatively free to pursue locations with high amenities or desirable political characteristics.

Agglomeration Economics and Factor Costs

The production of movies and other films (e.g., television commercials and promotional films) provides examples of an office-using industry oriented toward agglomeration economies and low production costs. This industry depends on the specialized skills of producers, actors, writers, set designers, and musicians. It also depends on specialized equipment and facilities (studios) for filming and editing filming. The skilled labor and facilities are available in a few locations, notably Los Angeles and New York. For example, a studio may be rented on short notice in these cities, whereas this is very difficult and very costly in most cities. Thus, the agglomeration economies available in a few cities make these cities low-cost locations for film production.

Transportation Costs

Commuting costs (i.e., the cost of transporting workers to the office, can be viewed as a component of agglomeration economies and factor costs). Transportation of outputs (i.e., decisions and information) from the office to users of office services is a more complex area. It includes the use of telecommunication facilities to convey office outputs over long distances. For example, teleconferencing facilities, E-mail (electronic-mail), fax machines, and computer bulletin boards all facilitate long-distance communication of office services.

The role of transportation costs is investigated in more detail in the discussion of economic base analysis later in this chapter. Chapter 5 examines the role of telecommunications in the decentralization of office activities.

Amenities and Political Factors

Some office firms, like some manufacturing firms, are "footloose"; their location is not determined primarily by factor costs, agglomeration economies, or transportation costs. Instead, they can seek locations that maximize the quality of life for those making the location decision. For example, research and development facilities are often free to select areas that have attractive climates; skilled labor can generally be obtained at lower costs in these areas. Financial services corporations are often concerned about political factors and exchange rate movements when they choose their locations on an international scale. Survey research has confirmed the way in which these factors guide international financial services firms to major metropolitan areas such as New York and London (Dunning and Norman 1987).

ECONOMIC BASE ANALYSIS

As mentioned previously, improvements in telecommunications have dramatically affected the location of office firms. To understand this, it is helpful to review a simple but useful method known as economic base (EB) analysis. This section discusses economic base theory and evidence for its application to office activities. It then investigates the implications of the theory for public policy designed to promote the growth of jobs and economic activity.

Economic base theory attempts to explain the growth and decline of employment and income within a local area. It focuses on a major source of growth and decline: exports of goods and services to other areas. The theory begins by taking total employment (TE) and dividing it into two parts: basic employment (BE) and nonbasic employ-

Figure 4.1 TOTAL EMPLOYMENT AND ECONOMIC BASE THEORY

Basic employment (BE)

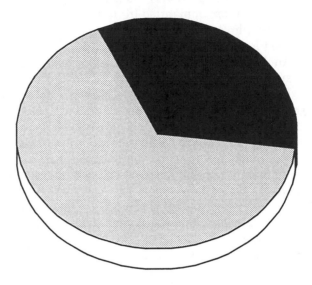

Nonbasic or service
related employment (NBE)

Notes: TE, total employment. Basic employment produces goods and services exported outside the local area. Nonbasic or local service-sector employment produces goods and services sold inside the local area. Changes in basic employment cause changes in nonbasic employment, not vice versa (the arrow runs only in one direction): $\Delta BE \rightarrow \Delta NBE$. Change in basic employment plus change in nonbasic employment adds up to change in total employment: $\Delta BE + \Delta NBE = \Delta TE$.

ment (NBE). This process can be viewed as taking a slice out of the pie of total employment (figure 4.1). The slice taken out is basic employment, whereas the rest of the pie is nonbasic employment.

Basic employment is important because it produces goods and services exported outside the local area. The sale of goods and services outside the local area brings money back into the area to pay for labor and other costs of production. Thus, the important thing about basic employment is that people inside the local area bring money in from the outside.

When exports grow, more money comes into the local area, thus

stimulating the local economy. If the increase in export sales is permanent, then more basic employees need to be hired to produce more
basic goods and services. Thus, basic employment grows (see the
shaded area in figure 4.1). As basic employment grows, more goods
and services are demanded from the local economy; that is, the extra
basic employees spend at least part of their money on items purchased locally.

An important tenet of economic base theory is that growth in
basic employment will stimulate growth in nonbasic employment.
Nonbasic employment is that part of employment that produces
goods and services for sale inside the local area. Nonbasic employees
can be found in restaurants, grocery stores, dry cleaners, and all
sorts of retail activity. The distinction between basic and nonbasic
employment rests on the fact that nonbasic employment does not
bring money into the local area (i.e., it does not export its goods and
services). The whole theory works in reverse. A decline in exports
will cause a decline in basic employment, which, in turn, will cause
a decline in nonbasic employment. Thus, the total pie will shrink.
In fact, the theory has been used to explain the development of ghost
towns as exports (e.g., of gold or silver) decline.

The most important feature of economic base theory is that changes
in basic employment (ΔBE) cause changes in nonbasic employment
(ΔNBE), not vice versa. For example, if the local restaurant sector
declines for some reason (e.g., food becomes more expensive), this
will not cause a decline in basic employment according to economic
base theory. In figure 4.1, this theoretical statement is represented
by the arrow that points from change in basic employment to change
in nonbasic employment. The theory simply says that the arrow does
not point back in the other direction.

Economic Base Theory and Office Markets: The Evidence

Beyers and Alvine (1985) and Marshall (1983) reversed one of the
standard assumptions used for empirical applications of economic
base (EB) analysis. EB models typically assume that manufactured
goods are exported and that business services are produced and
sold locally. These authors consider the possibilities that business
services export a considerable share of their product and that manufacturing locations are dependent on access to business services.
They use survey research to test the proposition that service employment does not export a significant quantity of output.

Using a sample of U.S. firms, Beyers and Alvine (1985) defined services to include detail from the following sectors: (1) transportation, communication, and utilities (TCU); (2) finance, insurance and real estate (FIRE); (3) business services such as advertising, computer services, research and development (R&D) laboratories, and management consulting; (4) other services such as legal, rental, accounting, and architectural. Their survey produced responses from 1,102 service firms in Seattle, Washington.

Beyers and Alvine's (1985) principal finding is that most service industries studied obtain less than half of their revenues from the local market. For all industries, 55.7 percent of revenues were nonlocal and 40.3 percent came from out of state or country. Exports were also high for computer firms, R&D laboratories, management consulting firms, public relations firms, architects, and engineers. Although Marshall (1983) did not report his findings in as much detail, the two studies are generally consistent. Given that one study is for the United States and the other for Britain, this suggests that they have found a general pattern of service exports.

A secondary finding of Beyers and Alvine (1985) is that small firms are just as likely to export services as large firms. The authors stated that this "totally defuses the notion that the small firm cannot be quite successful in obtaining spatially extensive business" (p. 23). They argue that public authorities should encourage small firms as well as large firms, and that service firms deserve attention as well as manufacturing firms.

Marshall (1982) advanced the hypothesis that the growth of manufacturing employment in British provincial areas (i.e., areas outside the greater London metropolitan region) is constrained by inadequate availability of business services. He cited a number of British studies purporting to show that provincial manufacturing firms: buy typing and employment-agency services locally; buy finance, market research, and computer services outside the local area; are more likely to import services if they are branches with headquarters elsewhere; and are more likely to buy services from within the organization if they are branch plants.

Marshall (1982) found that the percentage of business services purchased outside the manufacturing company depends on number of employees, single-site companies versus multisite status (head office or branch), and ownership (externally owned or independent). He maintained that organizational structure (e.g., externally owned or size class) can influence growth of business services and that the availability of business services in turn influenced growth of manufacturing employment.

The main conclusion of Marshall's (1982) study is that many business service firms export a substantial portion of their services. For example, computer services and management consulting export more than 75 percent of their services beyond a 10-mile radius. Even lawyers and accountants export 25 percent or 30 percent of their services. Likewise, van Dinteren (1987) found that Dutch office firms in medium-sized cities export similar percentages.

Marshall (1983) also found that most growth in employment in the business service sector is from in-situ expansion of employment (i.e., expansion at the same site). Furthermore, much of employment growth is in new firms (i.e., independent of a large organization) or in branch offices of firms with headquarters outside the region. Marshall did report some significant differences in business service growth by size of firm, with small firms showing some tendency to grow more rapidly than large firms.

Noyelle and Stanback, Jr. (1984) pointed out that most office employment has been separated spatially from manufacturing employment. In a service economy, office employment cannot be viewed as serving the needs of the manufacturing industry. Instead, office activities have taken on a productive role of their own, independent from the production of goods.

Other studies confirm Noyelle and Stanback, Jr.'s findings. They report no relationship between office employment and total employment. They also find that cities tend to specialize by type of office employment (e.g., banking, insurance, legal services, and so forth), so that there is considerable clustering of office employment by type across cities. Furthermore, they conclude that cities are tending to become more alike over time, where similarity is defined by the mix of office employment.

International Office Locations

A survey of international office locations has found evidence that factor costs and agglomeration economies (labor quality and cost, availability of support services, communications facilities, and market size) are important for branch office locations (Dunning and Norman 1987). Regional offices are more strongly influenced by internal organizational factors such as firm size or industry group. Furthermore, Dunning and Norman found evidence of a bandwagon effect in areas with established international offices.

Typically, the branch offices of foreign firms use their locations as a base for sales to other areas. For example, they may sell their goods or services to other regions within the country, or to other countries. Thus, they are typically involved in export activities. For this reason, growth in offices of foreign firms is usually associated with growth in basic employment.

Public Policy Implications of Economic Base Analysis

An obvious public policy implication of economic base analysis is that state and local government should seek to identify and attract basic employment in order to cause growth in the basic sector. This growth will then stimulate further growth in the nonbasic sector. Basic employment can be identified by industry or by firm. At the firm level, a simple approach is to target large firms as most likely to have basic employment. This is because a large concentration of employment in one firm (e.g., more than 500 employees) is not likely to be able to sell all of its goods and services within the local area. Thus, large firms usually export a large percentage of their output.

The use of large firms to identify basic employment gives a rough approximation. Beyers and Alvine (1985) conducted surveys indicating that small and medium-sized firms in many service industries export a substantial portion of their services (see discussion earlier in this chapter). Thus, it is desirable to supplement the large firm approach with a more detailed examination of all firms in some service industries.

It is often possible to identify industries that are likely to export a large percentage of their output. For example, it is well known that the Connecticut insurance industry services a worldwide clientele. Likewise, the aerospace industry typically sells products to governments and to airlines outside the area where they produce.

Public policy officials need to maintain a diversity of firms and industries in the basic sector. If basic employment is concentrated in one industry, decline in that industry will cause serious problems for the entire local economy. In fact, economic base theory has been used to explain the boom-town–ghost-town phenomenon that followed the discovery of gold. Thus, a wise policy is to develop a variety of basic industries.

URBAN ECONOMICS AND INTRAMETROPOLITAN LOCATION DECISIONS

Intrametropolitan location decisions cover the choice between the central business district (CBD) and the suburbs, as well as the choice of a specific location within each of these areas. For example, a suburban node of office supply—perhaps a satellite to the CBD— may provide an attractive location. These intrametropolitan location decisions are governed by the same list of five economic factors considered earlier in this chapter. However, the intrametropolitan decision puts greater emphasis on access to customers, on the commute to work, and on access to specialized information sources that can be obtained in the CBD or suburban office centers. Also, differences in rent, taxes, and labor costs are important within the metropolitan area. For example, several studies have found that wages of clerical and secretarial labor are about 15 percent higher in the CBD than in the suburbs (Clapp and Dorpalen 1989; Hamer 1974).

Urban economics has developed a formal model of the way in which location decisions are made within a metropolitan area. This theory asserts that national, regional, and divisional headquarters— as well as banks, other financial institutions, law firms, and accounting firms—can bid for the most central locations in the CBD (see figure 4.2). According to Heilbrun (1987: 118), all of these firms are "complementary in providing high-level business services that require daily contact between firms." Therefore, they need the central locations.

These firms are supported by related business services such as temporary secretarial agencies, courier services, maintenance and repair services, office equipment suppliers, bookkeepers, routine financial services, and the like. These "ancillary" services cannot afford the high rents paid on the most central class-*A* office space. Therefore, they are forced into class-*B* space or into less expensive, suburban office space. Thus, urban economics provides a simple framework for explaining the existence of clusters and zones of similar office activities (figure 4.2).

Note that neither of the two types of office activities in figure 4.2 could dominate the other by outbidding it for all locations. For example, suppose that the rent curve for ancillary services was shifted upward so that these services could outbid central office activities for the prime (i.e., most central) locations. This would be an impossible situation because then ancillary services would have no market for their services. Likewise, if the central office activities were able to outbid ancillary services for all locations, then there would be a lack of the latter services.

In addition to explaining broad patterns of land use, figure 4.2 provides a simple framework for highest- and best-use analysis. Typically, the land at any location goes to the highest bidder. The highest

Figure 4.2 URBAN ECONOMIES EXPLAIN BROAD PATTERNS OF LAND USE

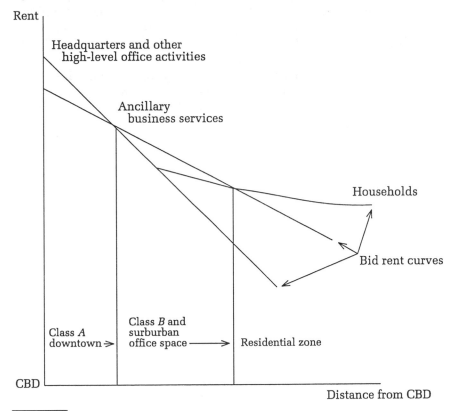

bidder is determined by the extent of need for agglomeration econo-mies available at the most central location. Agglomeration economies depend on interactions among various types of office activities: for example, administrative offices and ancillary services interact in fig-ure 4.2. In a real urban economy, a complex interaction occurs among different types of office activities (see chapter 5).

Why don't ancillary business services occupy the most central locations while headquarters and related offices occupy suburban office space? This cannot happen so long as the bid rent curve of headquarters is more steeply sloped than that of ancillary business services. The steep slope of the headquarters' bid rent (figure 4.2) derives from the urgency with which they need access to central facilities and information. Thus, the main insight of figure 4.2 is that some office firms have more urgent needs for the agglomeration economies associated with central locations; the process of bidding for space ensures that such firms will receive these locations and that ancillary services will be able to bid successfully only for peripheral locations.

In addition to explaining the location of office activities, urban economics explains the skyline of the city. As rent per square foot of office space rises toward the center of the city, it becomes profitable for developers to build at higher and higher densities. Thus, the tallest buildings would be found at the center of the city and the smaller buildings in the suburbs.

This story is easily modified to allow for a multinucleated city. Thus, clusters of relatively tall buildings can exist at subcenters at some distance from the CBD. Agglomeration economies explain suburban office clusters. The benefits from the agglomeration economies occur whenever two or more office activities interact. Suburban office clusters can develop enough of these interactions to provide substantial substitution for the agglomeration economies available in the CBD.

Suburbanization

The suburbanization of office space and office employment has been a major characteristic of office markets over the past 30 to 40 years. Urban economic theory explains this as a consequence of improvements in telecommunications and the shift of skilled labor to the suburbs. Both these factors have made the suburbs more attractive. For example, a temporary secretarial agency can now locate farther away from the CBD while communicating with clients by use of fax machines or by transmission of computer files over telephone lines. At the same time, skilled administrative employees and skilled secretarial labor can have relatively short commutes to the suburban office.

Margo (1992) presented evidence that 40–50 percent of all suburbanization of the population from 1950 through 1980 was caused by increases in real income. Since the locations of people and of jobs are tightly interconnected (people follow jobs and jobs follow people), one might expect that rising real income is an important source of suburbanization in the office market. Margo's results suggest that periods of slow growth in real income, such as the 1989–92 period, should be associated with slow suburbanization of office space. Further empirical work is needed to verify this.

The suburbanization of office employment provides part of the explanation behind the overbuilding of office space in the late 1980s (see Clapp, Pollakowski, and Lynford 1992). This follows from the difficulty that developers have in properly anticipating demand at each of many dispersed areas in the suburbs. Developers form their best estimates about the location of the greatest demand and build there. When they are wrong, vacancy may be high during an extended absorption period.

Pollakowski, Wachter, and Lynford (1992) examined office market dynamics in 21 metropolitan areas from 1981 to 1990. They tested a standard model of office market dynamics, emphasizing the roles of employment growth, the natural vacancy rate, and office construction responding after a lag. They found that estimated relationships are very different in Manhattan than in other submarkets. Furthermore, the larger metropolitan areas appear to be more closely related to standard explanatory variables than smaller areas. The authors speculated that the varying structures among office submarkets might be explained by the oversupply of institutional capital to those second- and third-tier markets that were the fastest growing during the first half of the 1980s.

Smith and Selwood (1983) used regression analysis to calculate density gradients for office floor space.[3] They reported a trend toward smaller (less-negative) gradients for each of six types of office sectors. Thus, office space has become more suburbanized along with office employment.

Daniels' (1977) study of major urban centers in England found that clerical employment was moving to suburban areas at a much greater rate than administrators, managers, and professional workers. The data support Daniels' contention that routine work benefits from lower rents, lower taxes, and greater availability of space in the suburbs, but that other office employees still depend on face-to-face contacts in the center. This theme is developed in greater detail in chapter 5.

Hedonic Rental Literature

In hedonic rental studies, rental rate is explained primarily by tenant, building, and locational characteristics. For example, a negative sign is expected when distance from a central point is regressed on rental rate (Brennan, Cannaday, and Colwell 1984; Clapp 1980). Clapp used access to suburban nodes of office space to capture the value of specialized office subcenters. Goddard (1975) and others have suggested that these specialized suburban nodes can substitute for some of the agglomeration economies in the downtown. More research is needed in this area; for example, access to specialized office concentrations (legal, financial, services, and so forth) could be included in the hedonic models.

In another study, Benjamin, Shilling, and Sirmans (1992) used data from Greensboro, N.C., to show that an increase in security deposits is associated with an increase in rental rates. Other lease provisions appear to be priced appropriately.

Wheaton (1984) sought to determine whether tenants or owners pay the property tax. He used a simultaneous-equation technique to estimate a model that explains market rent as a function of structural and locational variables. Thus, his findings are relevant to the suburbanization issue. Wheaton utilized data from leasing agents on office buildings in Boston. The dependent variable was the last recorded contract rate (within one year). His findings—that rent per square foot is negatively related to building age, positively related to square footage of floor space in the building, and positively related to the number of floors in the building—agree with most related studies. Like the Clapp (1980) study, Wheaton found a positive relationship with access to other office space surrounding the building (his RATIO variable).

Glascock, Jahanian, and Sirmans (1990) used building data for Baton Rouge to show that large buildings rent for more per square foot than small buildings. They also demonstrated that full-service buildings rent for more than partial service buildings and that Class-A space rents for more than Class-B space.

Use of Constant-Quality Rent Index

Wheaton and Torto (1992) developed a constant-quality index for office rents by regressing rents on various lease terms, building characteristics, locational characteristics, and variables for the time the lease was signed.[4] The lease, building, and locational characteristics are an attempt to control for the quality of the office space covered by the transactions. The time variables allowed Wheaton and Torto to track the change in constant-quality rents over time. Their data indicate that this constant-quality rent index can move opposite average rental rates. This occurs when the lease and property characteristics change substantially from one time period to another.

Miles and colleagues (1991) questioned the feasibility of constructing constant-quality price indexes for commercial real estate. They argued that incomplete disclosure, complex characteristics of each transaction, and few sales transactions make these indexes infeasible. Although Wheaton and Torto had a large number of lease transactions, they used simple approximations to complex lease, property, and locational characteristics.

Wheaton and Torto (1992) reported a general downward movement in real constant-quality rental rates from the late 1970s through 1990. When all rents are stated in terms of constant 1990 dollars, rental declines range from roughly $2 per square foot in Cincinnati and Washington, D.C., to about $8 per square foot in Houston. In several cities, real rents increased from the late 1970s to the early 1980s and then declined. Thus, the Wheaton and Torto study suggests possible insights into patterns of office markets cycles.

Wheaton and Torto (1992) also found that large buildings (those five or more stories high) typically command considerably more rent per square foot than smaller buildings. The premium for high buildings ranges from 6 percent in Houston to 10–13 percent in Denver, Cincinnati, and San Francisco. A number of other studies confirm that larger buildings command higher rents per square foot, but the literature does not agree on the reasons for this. The most common explanations are: (1) greater opportunities for face-to-face contact via the most convenient form of transportation, the elevator; (2) the prestige associated with the view from higher floors; and (3) prestige associated with well-known tenants who are attracted to the large amount of space available in larger buildings. These demand-side factors interact with the supply side: the marginal cost of construction rises as additional floors are added. These explanations are difficult to disentangle, but, conceivably, researchers will develop the data necessary to test one hypothesis against the other.

Wheaton and Torto (1992) found that the square footage covered by an individual lease has variable effects on rents per square foot. In some cities it has no effect, whereas in others it reduces rents. They hypothesized that there are two counteracting effects: (1) tenants negotiating for larger amounts of space have greater bargaining power (e.g., they are prestige tenants); or (2) the difficulty of assembling a large area in one building gives landlords greater bargaining power. These two forces cause rental rates to move in opposite directions, so the net effect on negotiated rents could be positive, zero, or negative.

Location is represented in the Wheaton and Torto (1992) study by selected ZIP codes.[5] In most markets, the authors found roughly a 50 percent range in rental rates from the worse location to the best location. In larger, newer markets such as Denver and Houston, they reported a 25–30 percent range in rents, whereas smaller markets such as Cincinnati have a 15–25 percent range.

Hedonic Studies for Architects and Planners

Thibodeau (1990) investigated the effect of a new office building (a single high-rise building in Dallas) on surrounding residential land values and found there was some negative effect on houses near the office building. It has been suggested that the negative effect occurs because of traffic congestion, air pollution, and reduction in sunlight. However, buildings from 1,000 meters to 2,500 meters from the office building experienced an increase in property values after the new high-rise was constructed, probably because of the building's positive effect on access to jobs. As distance increased from the new high-rise building, the circle of houses influenced by the building widened. Thus, many more houses were positively influenced by the building than negatively. The net effect of the high-rise building in Dallas was an increase in aggregate property values within a circle whose radius was 2,500 meters. Beyond this distance, the building had negligible effects on property values.

Vandell and Lane (1989) and Doiron, Shilling, and Sirmans (1992) have pointed out that special architectural features such as elaborate lobbies and atriums are expensive to produce. They asked whether the presence of these features adds enough to office rents to justify the costs of production. Both studies found that a significant increase in rental incomes accrued from the special architectural features in the sample of buildings they analyzed.

Doiron et al. (1992) furthermore built a model to evaluate the optimal quantity of special building features. In the case of office atriums, they recommended that architects and investors increase the size of the atrium to the point where the costs associated with an additional square foot of atrium space equal the additional rental income available because of the atrium. (costs include construction costs and lost revenue from the space used for the atrium). It would be feasible for architects and investors to approximate the kind of information needed to implement this model. However, the data on costs were not available to the authors.

Effect of Location on Lease Terms

Brennan and colleagues (1984) used logical relationships among lease terms in Chicago to formulate a model that explains rent in terms of location, building characteristics, tenant attributes, and lease terms. For example, they demonstrated that the greater the tenant responsibility for increases in building operating costs, the less base rent will be paid. They also found a positive relationship between square footage in the structure and base rent per square foot. In addition, the greater the distance from the most desirable streets in Chicago, the lower the rent.

As pointed out in chapter 1, the office lease is a complicated legal document involving extensive negotiation between the landlord and tenant. These negotiations deal with the amount of rent per square foot, increases in rent, and sharing of costs such as property taxes, insurance, and maintenance. Thus, the model by Brennan and colleagues (1984) may be viewed as a simple way of describing the trading that occurs when landlords and tenants negotiate.

Mills (1992) has argued that there is no reason why trade-offs are made only with respect to base rent. For example, a tenant who receives six months of free rent might be expected to give back something other than a higher initial (i.e., base) rent. Instead, this tenant might agree to pay larger increases in rent, or larger shares of taxes and insurance. Mills proposed that the dependent variable in the hedonic rental equation should be an estimate of the present value of all the payments under the lease, rather than base rent. Using a sample of Chicago buildings, he estimated present value of lease payments based on assumptions about the discount rate and the rate of inflation. He found that the present value of lease payments was strongly positively related to the size of the building and the availability of restaurants, banking, and health care near the building. On the other hand, building age and the vacancy rate in the building had strong negative effects on rental payments.

Mills (1992) computed the same regressions with the dependent variable used by Brennan and colleagues (1984): the asking rental rates per square foot of floor space. Surprisingly, he reported coefficients similar to those produced when the present value of all contract terms is included as the dependent variable. In Mills's judgment, this similarity cannot be explained by the assumptions (e.g., about expected inflation and the discount rate) made for the present-value calculations. Rather, he concluded that office tenants may fail to do the present-value calculations suggested by his model. Another possibility is that negotiations between landlords and tenants are simplified by trading base rent for other contract terms. Thus, any variable that influences the present value of lease payments may proportionally influence base rent. Finally, future research should evaluate whether the two dependent variables (asking rents and present value of all future payments) really yield the same conclusions about trade-offs among contract terms.

SUMMARY AND CONCLUSIONS

This chapter has summarized the literature on office location decisions at the regional and metropolitan levels. The fundamental factors that drive office locations include: agglomeration economies (access to specialized sources of information and specialized labor), the availability and cost of labor, the cost of maintaining contact with clients and other users of office services, political factors, and amenities such as climate and living costs. Improvements in telecommunications such as improved long-distance conference facilities and improved document transmission have encouraged office firms to move farther from the users of their services. This has enhanced the value of economic base analysis, which shows that increases in exports of office services imply local economic growth.

The hedonic pricing literature uses multivariate statistical analysis to assess the impact of location factors on office rents. This literature has clearly shown that office rents decline with distance from the CBD and that improved access to the homes of employees generally increases office rents. Higher property taxes have been shown to have some negative influence on base rents, whereas improved building amenities such as architecture have been found to have some positive influence on rents. Hedonic pricing models have been used to develop a constant quality rental index for office properties.

Economic theory provides a framework for explaining broad patterns of office location and changes over time in those locations. However, by working within a general theoretical framework, it has turned a blind eye to much institutional detail that is important for office location. Private parties (developers, lenders, investors, and the like) and public officials would like to know why a given type of office employment is particularly suited to a given location. For example, starting with a location in search of a user, is the location best suited for back office activities such as the computer operations division? Or is it best suited for a sales office? Or a research and development office? Economic theory has little to say in response to such questions.

The next chapter turns to the branch of the literature that deals more fundamentally with some of the issues ignored by economic analysis. This literature uses a very different empirical technique—survey research—to investigate the institutional landscape surrounding the location decision.

Notes

1. Of course, many location decisions are not this complex because the country (or region or city) is constrained by historical or political factors.

2. For a summary of this information, see Heilbrun (1987, chap. 4:2).

3. Density is the square footage of floor space divided by square footage of land. The density gradient is the change in density as distance from downtown increases.

4. Their rental rate is "consideration rent" defined in chapter 1.

5. They used ZIP codes where there were enough leases within a single ZIP code to allow the location effect to be distinguished.

Chapter Five

OFFICE LOCATIONS: THE ROLE OF FACE-TO-FACE CONTACTS

Chapter 4 used economic theory to identify and describe five major factors influencing office locations: agglomeration economies, factor costs, transportation costs (including commuting), political factors, and amenities. These five factors were then used as a framework for evaluating regional, international, and intermetropolitan location decisions.

Although the economic framework is useful, it is too broad for many applications, leaving specific questions unanswered that are pertinent to location decisions. Consider the needs, for example, of an engineering firm trying to make a location decision and of an official of the state Department of Economic Development who is assisting that firm. The information in chapter 4 would help the firm and the public official identify the major determinants of the location decision, but it does little to pinpoint individual characteristics that would be particularly attractive to the firm. This chapter investigates the importance of one specific characteristic—the potential for face-to-face contact—in office-location decisions.

Researchers in the fields of geography and planning have used surveys to develop specific linkages among different types of office activities. For example, Goddard (1973) showed that London engineering firms choose locations close to the locations of architects, finance, and banking employment. Goddard identified functional linkages by using a survey research technique known as "contact diaries," which record person-to-person contact over the telephone or face-to-face. Frequency of contacts can be correlated with location choices to identify a relationship between frequency of face-to-face contact and spatial clustering of office activities.

The contact patterns literature can be viewed as an elaboration of agglomeration economies. Recall that agglomeration economies are derived from access to specialized labor and facilities such as a courthouse or a stock exchange. Since telephoning can be done at low cost from virtually any distance, face-to-face contact is an important element of agglomeration economies for office activities.

The close relationship between agglomeration and face-to-face contacts has been studied by Daniels (1979) and others, using survey research, sometimes in the form of informal interviews with business executives. They have documented linkages in terms of face-to-face contacts. This chapter thus provides more detail on the face-to-face literature and its implications for office-location decisions.

FACE-TO-FACE CONTACTS: GLUE OF OFFICE MARKETS

The convenience of face-to-face contacts for the exchange of limited, ephemeral information has long been recognized by geographers and planners as an important force shaping the location and concentration of office employment. Over 30 years ago, Lichtenberg (1960) argued that corporate executives need to respond quickly to a large amount of changing, subtle, and elusive information, and that face-to-face contacts are the accepted means of obtaining (and, perhaps evaluating) this information. He concluded that high-level executives would be attracted to the centers of large cities.

Other authors have commented on the availability of relatively intense face-to-face contacts in central business districts (CBDs). For instance, Stanback, Jr., and Knight (1970) noted that the CBD offers rich opportunities for interaction in those cities that provide general office service to a region. Wabe (1966) found that the city center provides availability of meetings, including the convenience of meeting travelers from other areas; and Robbins and Terleckyj (1960) explained the concentration of securities industry employment in Manhattan's Wall Street area by the need for continual personal contact with those in the money market core. The latter authors pointed out that the need for costly direct telephone lines also ties the securities industry together.

Three Types of Face-to-Face Contacts

An influential study by Thorngren (1970) reviewed numerous articles on the decisionmaking process, distilling a model of decisions controlling the activities of organizations. He hypothesized that information and material flows are of three types. First, programmed processes use previously allocated resources to influence well-defined parts of the environment. Second, planning processes link information flows with flows of resources and money. Finally, orientation contacts explore previously unconnected parts of the environment. This model has guided survey research by Tornqvist (1970), Thorngren (1970), Goddard (1973), and Goddard and Morris (1976).

Hypotheses advanced by Goddard (1973), described earlier here, and by Tornqvist (1970) relate to the patterns of contact activity within and between organizations or occupations. They suggest that spatial patterns of employment locations are a consequence of patterns of contact activity. Tornqvist argued that information density governs agglomeration economies (i.e., the benefits from spatial concentration of employment and economic activity). These benefits include a group of skilled workers shared by many businesses, specialized transportation, and communication facilities (e.g., containerized cargo-handling facilities), access to retail and cultural amenities, and access to specialized sources of information such as courthouse documents, skilled accountants, and financial analysis. Thus, agglomeration economies are related, in part, to the intensity of face-to-face contacts with employees, customers, and information sources.

Tornqvist (1970) identified contact intensity with time spent in face-to-face contacts and number of contacts per employee per unit of time. He found a strong positive statistical association between time spent in contacts and salary (or job status). Tornqvist was not specific with respect to the locational implications of contact intensity, whereas Lichtenberg (1960) and Evans (1973) emphasized the importance of contacts for interregional location decisions.

Intraurban Contact Patterns

Robbins and Terleckyj (1960) pointed out that relocation from Wall Street would be prohibitive for a single securities firm because of agglomeration economies. As an example of agglomeration, the processing of checks and stock certificates requires centrally located clerical jobs (Lichtenberg 1960). Robbins and Terleckyj (1960) argued that external economies result from a variety of skilled services that are available in a small area. Similarly, evidence of direct personal contact with a large variety of economic activities was cited by Tornqvist (1970: 29); even with his aggregated occupational classifications, the executives and administrators who accounted for 40 percent of all personal contacts had a little more than half of their contacts outside their own group.

It is plausible that contact variety generally diminishes with increasing distance from the CBD, but the evidence for this is still largely impressionistic. Thorngren (1970) mentioned the need for executives to access a wide variety of functions in the central city. Rannels (1956) indicated that firms locating in the city center benefit from the "nearness to establishments with which they have linkages and by the availability of services of all kinds which they require" (p. 55). Burns (1977) stated that a variety of specialized services "are most readily available in metropolitan areas and particularly in central cities" (p. 211).

Goddard (1973), following methodology developed by Tornqvist (1970), created very general status groups from the managerial occupations included in his survey of face-to-face contacts in London. There were fairly wide variations in the number of telephone contacts and meetings recorded in the three-day periods during which the contact diaries were kept. In general, the higher-status occupations had a greater number of face-to-face meetings. The evidence on telephone contacts was more mixed, but the highest status group (managing director, chairman, or senior partner) had at least 20 percent more telephone contacts than any other group. This generally confirms the findings of Thorngren (1970) and of Tornqvist (1970), and it supports the three levels of information flows discussed in the previous subsection.

Some office occupations can partially satisfy their contact needs by clustering in less-centralized locations. The existence of office clusters was confirmed by Goddard (1968; 1973), who measured the amount of floor space classified by industry type, in each cell of a grid imposed on central London. Cluster analysis revealed reasonable patterns. Cluster analysis was then applied to a to-from communication matrix developed from the contact diaries. Two of the clusters formed by the contacts (banking and civil engineering) closely paralleled the spatial clustering. Deviations in the other clusters appeared to be related to the small sample size for the contact diaries: the spatial clusters generally made more sense than the functional clusters.

Goddard's work suggests that banking and finance (including clearing banks but not stockbrokers) can outbid civil engineering and other office functions for the most central locations: banking tends to be located in the old City of London, whereas civil engineering is more concentrated in Westminster and Bloomsbury. Goddard's study of trips by taxi and walking (57 percent of all business trips in central London) indicated that personal contacts are important within *and between* these geographical clusters (1975). He concluded that "some activities are clearly tied not only to the city at large but to particular subareas within it. These subareas or office districts appear to be maintained by a strong pattern of internal circulation" (1975: 34).

Locational Change: Suburbanization and Deconcentration

Smith and Selwood (1983) used regression analysis to calculate density gradients for office floor space. They revealed a trend toward declining gradients for each of six types of office sectors. Since the density gradient is the rate of change of floor space per acre of land, a declining gradient indicates suburbanization of office space.

Daniels' (1977) study of major urban centers in England found that clerical employment had been moving to suburban areas at a much greater rate than administrators, managers, and professional workers. Daniels' data support the contention that routine work benefits from lower rents, lower taxes, and greater availability of space in the suburbs, but that other office employees still depend on face-to-face contacts in the center.

Daniels (1982) reported a survey sponsored by the Manchester (England) City Council and completed by a senior person in each of 1,520 offices in that city. The results showed that office locations are determined primarily by: (1) easy access to clients, customers, or services; (2) availability of office premises; (3) prestige; (4) ability to obtain suitable staff; (5) rent and local taxes. The first two factors were mentioned by 50 percent or more of the firms surveyed, whereas the latter three were mentioned by 35–42 percent of firms surveyed. In addition, proximity to hotels, shopping, and entertainment was mentioned by 11 percent of firms.

These results are compatible with the results of a survey of London by Rhodes and Kan (1971), who focused on cost savings (in rents, property taxes, staff costs, communications costs, and operating costs) for moves from central London. They found that the average firm saved 25 percent of total operating costs, even after experiencing some increase in communications costs. However, 85 percent of the moves studied were partial moves, involving only part of the firm; sales and head-office functions tended to remain in London to deal with communications needs. Similarly, the London-based Location of Offices Bureau found that 35 percent of clients mentioned economy (savings on rent) as a reason for considering decentralization. About

27 percent mentioned the need to expand; an equal proportion mentioned related factors: expiration of a lease and/or demolition (15–17 percent); and integration with other parts of the organization (10–12 percent).

Using Survey Research to Evaluate Public Policy

A methodology for evaluating public policy designed to redistribute office activities has been developed in England. Hardman (1973) recognized that offices function as part of an interdependent communications network, and that when one office moves to the suburbs, communications damage hurts firms that remain. Hardman conducted a comprehensive survey designed, in part, to measure communications damage in terms of travel time away from the office and abandonment of some face-to-face meetings. His findings support the notion that substantial communications damage can occur.

Contact diaries can be used to evaluate the travel costs associated with maintaining face-to-face contacts at the same level and location as before a move to the suburbs (Clapp 1983; Pye 1977). These authors argued that public policy can be evaluated in terms of changes in total costs, primarily costs to maintain face-to-face contacts, wages, rents, and property taxes.

A similar methodology was applied to a suburbanization policy implemented by the City of Toronto Planning Board in 1975. The Toronto policy was premised on a redundancy of office activities in the downtown and on the notion that many offices would be more productive in the suburbs. Code (1979) combined survey information on face-to-face contacts among downtown Toronto firms and information on transportation costs and time. For a given office industry (e.g., life insurance companies, engineering consultants, and so forth), he calculated the cost (including time cost valued at the average Toronto salaries and bonuses for low-to-middle management personnel) of maintaining the same level of face-to-face contacts downtown after the move to the suburbs. These costs were divided by the average square footage occupied by the office industry. The result was an estimate of the minimum rent difference between suburb and downtown required to induce the average firm in the industry to move to the suburbs. Code acknowledged that the quality of face-to-face contacts was omitted from this approach.

The main conclusion of Code's (1979) analysis was that the minimum rent differences required to move to the suburbs in 1979 were much greater than rent differences that existed in 1979. The most mobile activities (i.e., those requiring the smallest rent difference to move to the suburbs) were life insurance, engineering consultants, oil companies, manufacturing head-offices, and business finance firms. The least mobile activities were construction engineering consultants, actuaries, civic associations, customs brokers, and investment dealers.

Another survey of Toronto conducted by Code (1983) covered 1,159 large office firms. Again, the information was aggregated by industry. The study's main conclusion was that relocation from the downtown to the suburbs had decreased steadily from 1960 to 1977. By the end of this period, over 70 percent of relocation in the suburbs originated in other suburban locations. Thus, public policy designed to stimulate moves to the suburbs had reached a point of diminishing returns.

Statistical Tests of Role of Face-to-Face Contacts

Clapp (1980) included distance from the downtown in a regression on asking rents at the building level. In his model, distance is a proxy for access to customers and to specialized sources of information. He found a statistically significant negative association between distance and rents after controlling for other factors such as taxes and building characteristics. The problem with this test is that distance might proxy for other factors such as availability of land for commercial construction. Thus, the test does not prove conclusively that face-to-face contacts are important.

Clapp (1980) also developed more-direct tests of one type of face-to-face contact: access to the homes of workers. Using a survey instrument, he measured the average commuting time to each building in the sample for a typical employee in the building.[1] Average commuting time was found to be negatively related to rents and was related to distance in the expected U-shaped manner (i.e., the most distant locations, as well as the most central locations, were less accessible to employees than intermediate locations). This test provided some direct evidence that one form of face-to-face contact, access to employees, is a factor in the determination of office rents.[2] Since rents are an important factor in the location decision, it follows that commuting time does influence these decisions.

Archer (1981) used a survey instrument to measure three kinds of face-to-face contact: linkages to accountants, lawyers, and specialized services; commuting to work; and access to markets. He used a choice model (known as a "logit" model) in which the dependent variable was a choice between the downtown and the suburbs (i.e., the depen-

dent variable had values of zero [for suburbs] or one [for downtown]).
Archer found that this choice was not significantly influenced by
linkages to specialized services, but that it was significantly influenced by access to markets and to employees.

Long and colleagues (1984) used the need for face-to-face contacts
as the basis for developing hypotheses about the determinants of
intrametropolitan location choice. Their logit regression explained
firm location (probability of locating in a given subarea) with variables drawn from survey results for office users in the Hartford metropolitan area. The survey included ratings for the importance of space
costs, amenities (e.g., access to shopping, restaurants, museums, and
theaters), accessibility, parking, and other characteristics. They combined this with information from the U.S. Census and other sources
on towns in the area. Their study was confined to public-sector
variables and face-to-face contacts; no building characteristics were
included.

Long and colleagues (1984) reported that the probability of locating
in an area was negatively influenced by property taxes and was
positively associated with amenities, provision of business services,
fire protection, and/or police protection. They interpreted the coefficients on two variables to mean that traffic congestion has a negative
influence on the probability that an office firm will locate in that
local area. The number of face-to-face meetings by professional
employees (but not other employees) was found to influence location
in the expected way. Thus, this was the first study to demonstrate
statistically that face-to-face contacts are significant determinants of
location behavior.

Ihlanfeldt and Raper (1990), building on Clapp (1980, 1988), con-
nected the contact patterns literature with cross-sectional tests of
intermetropolitan location. The contact patterns literature argues that
there is a major difference between the location choices for new firms
and those for existing firms that are relocating. Existing firms have
substantial relocation costs, whereas newly formed office businesses
can choose a location without large moving costs or interruption
of business contacts. Ihlanfeldt and Raper found evidence for their
hypothesis that the presence of support services (e.g., secretarial and
accounting services) was more important in attracting new independent firms than new branches of existing firms. Raper and Ihlenfeldt's
essay at the end of this volume gives examples of these findings and
neatly develops a major theme of this monograph—that institutional
detail is vitally important for location decisions.

Like Archer (1981) and Long and colleagues (1984), Ihlanfeldt and

Raper (1990) used a choice model, but their choice was at the Census tract level, whereas the previous authors had examined the choice among towns in the CBD and suburbs. Ihlanfeldt and Raper indicated that both new independent and new branch firms were influenced in the expected way by wages, access to customers, land costs, access to public transportation, and access to restaurants and entertainment. Tax rates were not influential in their sample. In addition, new independent firms were strongly linked spatially to suppliers of support services, whereas this was not the case for new branch firms. Thus, Ihlanfeldt and Raper's results confirm an "incubator" hypothesis that says that locations that provide services needed by new firms will have a competitive advantage in attracting office employment.[3]

CRITIQUE OF CONTACT PATTERNS LITERATURE

Most of this literature has been protected from detailed criticism by its status as pioneering work, blazing new trails in unchartered territory. In this context, use of survey research has been not only skillful but highly appropriate. By providing information on the way institutions and decision processes work, these studies have laid the groundwork for subsequent research. However, the overall influence of this literature has been limited. Not only has it emphasized casual empiricism, intuition, and general agreement among authors not working independently, but the general propositions that emerge from models, such as central place theory, have not been formed into a coherent framework. Thus, the structure necessary to develop an organized literature with incremental additions to the body of knowledge has not formed. These weaknesses are reflected in the very limited ability of this research to reach policy conclusions. For example, Goddard (1973) was guarded in his recommendations with respect to the British policy of dispersing office jobs away from London. Lacking a theoretical framework, the assumptions underlying policy recommendations cannot be tested. As another example, Marshall's 1983 study contains several drawbacks in this regard. First, it examined variables pair-wise, so joint effects of multiple explanatory variables are impossible to determine. For instance, the effect of firm size and organizational control (externally owned versus independent) cannot be examined simultaneously from his published findings. Methodologies such as those used by Clapp (1980), Long et al. (1984), and Ihlanfeldt and Raper (1990) could remedy this.

Second, Marshall (1983) used chi-square tests and Mann-Whitney U-statistics to test for the effect of organizational structure on markets for business services. Yet, this methodology lacks any form of interdependency between supply and demand. From the point of view of simultaneous-equation econometric models, the supply and demand sides have not been identified (see chapter 3). Therefore, Marshall's methodology is incapable of determining whether lack of business services has constrained the spatial pattern of manufacturing employment. Apparently unaware of these limitations, Marshall argued for government policy to stimulate the location of business services in the provinces.

A third drawback of Marshall's (1983) study is that his findings do not strongly support his main conclusions. For example, some 36 percent of the sales of the typical business service activity were to the manufacturing sector. Yet, it is questionable whether this percentage is large enough to determine the bulk of employment growth in business services. Also, the fact that most employment growth is from in-situ expansion in independent or branch offices says nothing about growth due to sales to manufacturing firms as opposed to sales to other firms.

Beyers and Alvine (1985) were more cautious than Marshall in drawing conclusions. Nevertheless, by focusing on organizational structure, they ignored a large number of variables that influence exports and growth of firms. For example, their findings might reflect an economic climate that encouraged exports; the sales, and the exports, of small firms could be extremely sensitive to the business cycle. Thus, their findings should be viewed as suggestive of further research, particularly of multivariate hypothesis testing.

FORECASTS BASED ON CONTACT PATTERNS ANALYSIS

Goddard and Morris (1976) and Goddard and Marshall (1983) contended that telecommunications will eventually erode the need for face-to-face contact. They pointed to laboratory experiments indicating that face-to-face meetings are not substantially more effective than telephone conferencing supplemented by document transmission technology, and further cited evidence that the less-contact-intensive office functions have moved out of British CBDs. Pascal (1987), reporting similar evidence for U.S. cities, has argued that the "era of the computer and the communication satellite is inhospitable to the high density city" (p. 599). He applied the law of entropy to conclude that there will be a tendency toward complete areal uniformity in employment and population density.

On the other side of this issue, Clapp (1983) has argued that the subtleties of face-to-face contact cannot be matched by telecommunications. Furthermore, experiments by Short, Williams, and Christie (1976) indicated that face-to-face meetings are considered a warmer medium than telecommunications. Therefore, a social animal may elect to use telecommunications to enjoy even greater centrality rather than less.

Daniels (1986) summarized the views of geographers who argue that telecommunications may produce counterintuitive effects, actually promoting centralization. He stated that headquarters, regional offices, publishing, and broadcasting services may continue to have a major need for centrality to conduct face-to-face meetings and to service large telecommunications infrastructure. These activities may create a crossroads of telecommunication activity. Daniels (1986) cited evidence that office managers have not been aggressive about adopting telecommunications technology. Cost undoubtedly inhibits development of telecommunications. Thus, he concluded that we must be cautious about any forecast based on the effect of telecommunications on urban form. He regarded transportation costs (e.g., energy costs) as more important.

Rosen's essay at the end of this volume considers telecommunications along with other factors when forecasting office space per employee and total space to the year 2000.

SUMMARY AND CONCLUSIONS

The contact patterns literature views face-to-face contacts as a fundamental driving force behind office locations. These face-to-face contacts take three forms. First, programmed processes are routine contacts following well-defined channels. Second, planning processes use information to allocate resources so as to achieve previously defined goals. Finally, orientation contacts involve general, exploratory meetings. Successful orientation contacts define new objectives and new ways to use resources. Specific types of contacts are influential in the location choice. For example, the more routine the programmed contacts, the more likely is a remote location. In the extreme, very routine contacts can occur at a great distance from the users of the information produced by those contacts: for example, U.S. airline reservations can be processed in Ireland. Furthermore, changes in the cost of face-to-face contact cause changes in location decisions. For example, reduction in transportation costs causes more remote locations for routine contacts.

Choice models evaluate the effect of various explanatory variables on the choice of location. For example, access to customers is clearly an important factor in the choice between the CBD and suburbs. Also, access to public transportation, the cost of labor, and land costs are all factors influencing location choice. Ihlanfeldt and Raper (1990) have recently indicated that new independent office firms are linked to suppliers of support services, whereas this is not true for new branches of existing office firms. Thus, an incubator effect appears to be working in the office market. Raper and Ihlanfeldt develop this theme in the larger context of institutional structure (e.g., size and industry affiliation) in their essay at the end of this book.

The theory that face-to-face contacts play an important role in regional and intrametropolitan location decisions has been used to forecast the future of the office market. It seems plausible that improvements in telecommunications (e.g., greater availability of fax machines, electronic mail, and increasing investment in long-distance conference facilities) will influence the location of office firms. In particular, the availability of these telecommunications facilities in small to medium-sized cities will make these cities more attractive as locations for office activities. Increasing availability of telecommunication facilities may have made office firms more "foot-lose." Now they may be able to select a location based primarily on factor costs (rents, wages, and taxes) and only secondarily on access to clients. Improved telecommunications facilities in small to medium-sized cities may mean that office employment will continue to disperse from very large cities toward smaller cities. However, the timing and extent of the dispersion of office activities is open to question. Face-to-face contact may continue to play a central role despite greater availability of telecommunication facilities. Not only is face-to-face contact a warm medium that appeals to a social animal, but legal and institutional constraints may retard the influence of telecommunications on office growth and location.

Comparison of Economics and Contact Patterns Literature

The contact patterns literature and the economics literature consider issues relevant to locational changes, but they have been largely unaware of each other. Both branches have important contributions to make, and both have weaknesses. It appears that there is considerable complementarity in the methods that each uses. For example, economics models typically assume optimizing behavior. The possibility that institutional constraints govern the decision process is rarely considered. Similarly, markets are typically assumed to be in equilibrium. These assumptions simplify the analysis, but the sensitivity of the findings to the assumptions is open to question. The economics literature also ignores much of the complexity of historical and institutional forces that shape office markets. Simplistic armchair assertions are likely to substitute for detailed analysis based on survey research. For example, this literature has failed to learn from questionnaires about institutional constraints such as form of ownership, percentage of staff involved in clerical functions, or type of contact needs. A hedonic study including such explanatory variables might be able to significantly improve on previous research.

The contact patterns literature, on the other hand, has focused too narrowly on surveys; more breadth should stimulate creativity (Gould 1980). The survey results need to be organized into consistent theory, and more sophisticated statistical tools are required to test hypotheses and draw policy conclusions. For example, the assertion that communications damage can be evaluated through transportation cost estimates needs to be tested. Simultaneous equation methodology, as applied in some of the hedonic rental models, would appear appropriate. Similarly, the influence of the size or form of the organization on suburbanization could be evaluated statistically.

Notes

1. Since the survey was administered in elevators during times of heavy traffic, the interviewers felt that they obtained a random sample from all levels of the office hierarchy.

2. Access to employees may well be the most important form of face-to-face contact, because the commute to work is repeated every workday. This contributes to a significant trend bringing jobs closer to homes.

3. Ihlanfeldt and Raper (1990) pointed out that nearly half of all job growth during a four-year period was from the formation of new firms rather than the growth of existing firms. Thus, the ability to attract new office firms is an important part of public policy designed to stimulate local business activity.

Chapter Six

APPLICATIONS TO FORECASTS OF DEMAND, SUPPLY, AND RENTS

This chapter examines how selected research reviewed in previous chapters can be applied to forecasts and projections for the office market. The specific variables I want to forecast are related to demand (change in occupied square footage), office employment, supply (new construction), vacancy rates, rents, operating expenses, and net operating income. Forecasts of these variables—even highly imperfect forecasts—would be of great value to lenders, investors, developers, tenants, and other actors in office markets.

Since no one knows the future with certainty, forecasting is a controversial topic. Nevertheless, real estate decisions require some predictions about future events. This is most obvious with development decisions (e.g., new construction) where costs and revenues extend for many years. But it also applies to lending and investment decisions, since these commitments are generally long term.

The terms *forecasting* and *projection* should be used with caution. No one can predict the future with a high degree of accuracy. The best anyone can do is estimate *a* probable future, one of many possible future outcomes, or a range of probable outcomes. A reputable forecast or prediction is an estimate based on existing information. Risk is indicated by optimistic and pessimistic estimates.

This chapter begins with two approaches to forecasting the demand for office space. The first, developed by Kelly (1983) and by Clapp (1989), uses employment forecasts to forecast the demand for office space. The second approach, which is more complex, was developed by Birch (1986) and breaks down employment forecasts by office-using industries. (Rosen's essay at the end of this volume expands upon the Birch approach and provides forecasts on the U.S. office market to the year 2000.) The chapter then analyzes the supply side, including projections based on building-permit applications and the "pipeline" of proposed and under-construction projects. This part of the chapter also covers projections for rents, operating expenses, and vacancy rates. Forecasts and projections useful to practitioners need to be specific about *where* the projected changes will occur. Therefore, this chapter also looks at the implications of the spatial patterns literature for office market dynamics.

The final and most important part of this chapter explores the use of market analysis to evaluate the risks associated with lending, development, and investment in the office market. Risk analysis uses results from market analysis to alter projections. A range of reasonable alternatives can be examined to obtain optimistic to pessimistic forecasts on the future of a specific office investment or development. Risk analysis is most important because the failure to do adequate risk analysis has resulted in overbuilding and excessive lending.

DEFINING ABSORPTION

Absorption analysis typically provides data on the number of real property units (square feet of commercial space or number of residential units) sold or rented per month in the market area. Ideally, absorption would be defined as the net change in space actually occupied by tenants or owners; sometimes it is defined as the gross amount of space occupied during a given time period. But in practice, actual occupancy is often difficult to obtain, so this chapter uses information on sold or leased space minus space vacated by previous owners or tenants. When dealing with aggregate market absorption, one should not count preleased, presold, or subleased units as units absorbed, for three reasons. First, prelease or presale contracts can often be canceled at little cost to the tenants or buyers, so they don't represent final sales or leasing contracts. Second, preleased or sold space is not subtracted from the current vacant inventory. The purpose of absorption analysis is to determine how fast current inventory can be marketed. Third, it would be double counting to include presales as absorption and then to include the final sales as absorption; only final sales should be counted as absorption. Similarly, subleased space would double count space leased under the master contract. For these reasons, absorption numbers should represent final sales, final leases, and master leases, not subleases.

Finding and Using Absorption Information

The source of the absorption estimate may be field experience such as a windshield survey of vacant space, or a more careful canvas of buildings. Alternatively, absorption information can be obtained from conversations with professionals in the local market. In practice, however, the data underlying the absorption number are rarely presented in a way that allows the analyst to determine whether the monthly absorption rate applies to the subject property. This chapter proposes a solution to this problem by showing how the absorption data obtained from field surveys can be both presented so that the decision maker has a rich body of information on market trends and manipulated with spreadsheet software so as to provide information on variables that influence the absorption rate positively and negatively.

LONG-TERM DEMAND PROJECTIONS

The Clapp (1989) Approach

The Clapp (1989) approach is based on a simple, intuitively appealing proposition: Commercial space (e.g., class-*A* office space downtown) serves the needs of employees, so the rate of absorption (i.e., new space demanded) depends on the number of new employees of a given type entering the local market. Similarly, condominium absorption depends on population growth and on the age and family composition of the population.

Using employment growth to motivate the approach, if the number of new employees occupying office space increases by 10 percent, then one would expect absorption to increase by 10 percent. In the long run, growth in absorption cannot be substantially greater than growth in new employment. Although there are significant time periods when absorption is greater than employment growth, I argue here that this may be symptomatic of problems that adversely influence the investment and collateral value of the property.

As an example, consider finance, insurance, and real estate (FIRE) employment in Hartford. FIRE employment is used to form an index representing the growth in office employment because we lack a sufficiently long time series on employment in Hartford offices; the index of demand growth is used to estimate and forecast absorption of office space. FIRE employment serves to illustrate a method that can be applied in substantially the same way to any demand segment—for instance, to household groups such as young singles and empty nesters, who demand condominium or apartment units.

Demand Parameters and Absorption

Several variables other than employment or population are related to absorption. Two variables are related to the supply side: vacancy and new construction. If vacancy rates and/or new construction rates are low compared to employment growth, then the density of workers in existing space will rise. This causes rising rents and declining vacancy, which stimulates new construction. If vacancy rates are very low (e.g., less than 5 percent), then employment growth may create pent-up demand that will expand into new space as it becomes available.

Conversely, high vacancy rates and declining effective rents may cause employment to spread out, with each employee occupying more square footage. In this case, absorption rates may be higher than employment growth. However, this is a temporary situation accompanied by conditions that are unfavorable to the value of property: eventually, rents, construction, and property value will decline.

Consider what happens to absorption and collateral value in a soft market, when vacancy rates are high and effective rents are declining. Absorption will exceed employment growth because there are changes in square footage of floor space per employee. This ratio is called a ''demand parameter.'' Increases in square footage per employee can cause absorption to increase even when employment growth is zero or negative.

This represents a risky situation to lenders, developers, and investors. For example, in many cities in the United States since 1985, general-purpose class-A office vacancy rates have been high and rising and rents have been declining. This has caused office firms to expand the amount of space they use per employee and to lease extra space for future growth. Absorption rates have been higher than the rate of growth of office-using employment.[1] At the same time, the collateral value of office space has plummeted.

This example emphasizes that high absorption relative to employment growth is not always a favorable sign for those involved in supplying space (lenders, developers, investors). The risk is that a soft office market will result in high vacancy and low effective rents. In addition, *future* demand is being satisfied *now*. In those parts of the United States with excess supply, this means that rapid office employment growth will be required to absorb currently vacant or under-construction space, except in special circumstances.

Likewise, absorption can decrease when rents rise and businesses conserve on square footage per employee. These decreases are less

Figure 6.1 USE OF EMPLOYMENT GROWTH PROJECTIONS AND DEMAND
PARAMETERS TO PRODUCE ABSORPTION ESTIMATES

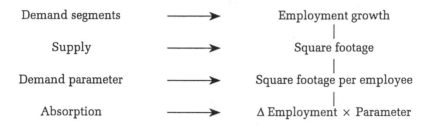

likely to have a detrimental effect on property value, for the reason
that decreases are usually associated with shortages of space and
rising rents. Firms delay the acquisition of space temporarily; eventually, they will need to expand space per employee. In this situation,
those backing new projects will usually find the market adequate to
ensure the safety of the investment. However, lenders or other clients
should be aware that absorption rates may be slower than the rate
of growth of office-using employment.

These methods for absorption analysis are based primarily on forecasts of changes in employment. Detailed forecasts of demand parameters are not attempted here. Nevertheless, I advocate conservative
estimates of these parameters (i.e., biased downward), which should
allow for adverse changes in the demand parameters during the
period following soft-market conditions, as well as for changes in
taste or technology that might cause an adverse change in the demand
parameters. This chapter's absorption estimates are not intended to
accurately forecast absorption, but, rather, to provide a conservative
basis for valuation decisions.

Absorption Forecasts

Figure 6.1 gives an overview of the proposed methodology for absorption forecasts. This methodology begins with data (at annual inter-
vals) on office employment in the local office market and then proceeds to use the limited information available from the following
sources: U.S. Department of Commerce, Bureau of Economic Analysis
(BEA), *BEA Regional Projections* (volume 2) in *Metropolitan Statistical Area Projections to 2035*); local brokers and consultants specializing in office space and usage; and town hall records on new construction of office space. The method includes four steps:

1. Find a demand parameter from historical data: square footage per employee.
2. Use a forecast, such as a third-party forecast, of office employment.
3. Make a conservative estimate of changes in the demand parameter, square footage per employee. Conservative estimates will give low absorption estimates.
4. Multiply estimated new employees by square footage per employee to obtain an estimate of the absorption of square footage.

Use of Employment Index When Data Are Inadequate

This section uses annual data for the years 1978–85, on total square footage and vacancy rates in class-*A* office space in downtown Hartford. The analysis was performed in 1986. However, I could not obtain the total number of office employees in that space, so I could not derive space per employee: the demand parameter is missing.

To offset the missing information on employment and space per employee, I propose using an employment index here as a proxy for office employment. Studies have shown that 95 percent of FIRE employment is in office buildings and that 40 percent of all office employment is in the FIRE sector. Therefore, I use FIRE employment in the broad Hartford /New Britain/ Bristol area as an index of employment in class-*A* office space. This index and a forecast of the index (line 5, table 6.1) is from the Connecticut Department of Labor (DOL).

The vacancy rate on class-*A* downtown office space (line 2, table 6.1) is from the same source as total square footage (line 1, table 6.1): the Farley Company, a major commercial brokerage firm. Occupied square footage is derived in the usual way from total square footage and the vacancy rate (line 3 is calculated from line 1 multiplied by line 2). Finally, absorption (line 4) is the change in occupied square footage.

To forecast absorption, the employment index (line 5, table 6.1) is related to absorption. The model does this very simply by dividing occupied square footage by employment: the last line of table 6.1 is line 3 divided by line 5. Square footage per employee is the demand parameter in this model, because it relates employment to the demand for office space. As will be seen, this demand parameter is a key element in the forecast.

To forecast to 1990 and 1995 (recall that the analysis was done in 1986), a projection is needed of the demand parameter (line 6,

Table 6.1 ABSORPTION ESTIMATED FROM OFFICE SPACE AND VACANCY: 1978–95 (SQUARE FOOTAGE AND EQUIPMENT IN THOUSANDS)

	Actual								Forecast	
	1978	1979	1980	1981	1982	1983	1984	1985	1990	1995
Total square footage	6,650.0	7,190.0	7,635.0	8,300.0	9,480.0	10,860.0	13,160.0	14,380.0	NA	NA
Occupancy rate (1 – vacancy)	94.6	97.2	95.8	93.1	92.7	90.4	88.5	84.7	NA	NA
Occupied square footage	6,290.9	6,988.7	7,314.3	7,727.3	8,788.0	9,817.4	11,646.6	12,179.9	17,584.0	23,091.4
Absorption (annual)	NA	697.8	325.6	413.0	1,060.7	1,029.5	1,829.2	533.3	1,080.8	1,101.5
Employment index (FIRE)	54.3	57.1	60.3	62.8	65.6	67.2	67.7	69.0	80.0	87.7
Occupied square footage/ employment index	115.9	122.4	121.3	123.0	134.0	146.1	172.0	176.5	219.8	263.3

Source: Index of employment and forecast of the index are from Connecticut Department of Labor and are for the Hartford/New Britain/ Bristol area.

Note: Data are for total square footage and vacancy rates in class-A office space in downtown Hartford. NA: not applicable.

Table 6.2 SENSITIVITY ANALYSIS: PESSIMISTIC DEMAND PARAMETERS
(SQUARE FOOTAGE PER EMPLOYEE [IN THOUSANDS] GROWS AT 2.9 PER YEAR)

	Actual			Forecast	
	1983	1984	1985	1990	1995
Total square footage	10,860.0	13,160.0	14,380.0	NA	NA
Occupancy rate (1 − vacancy)	90.4	88.5	84.7	NA	NA
Occupied square footage	9,817.4	11,646.6	12,179.9	15,280.0	18,022.4
Absorption (annual)	1,029.5	1,829.2	533.3	620.0	548.5
Employment index (FIRE)	67.2	67.7	69.0	80.0	87.7
Occupied square footage/ employment index	146.1	172.0	176.5	191.0	205.5

table 6.1). This parameter grew steadily over the eight-year historical period. Two factors contributed to this: first, increasing demand for corporate headquarters employment, a demand segment that requires a relatively large amount of space per employee; second, deteriorating market conditions over the period (note that occupancy rates declined).[2] As noted earlier, the softer market conditions that existed toward the end of the 1978–85 period typically caused increased absorption. Relatively plentiful space and discount pricing led firms to demand a large amount per employee.

Trends in the demand parameter, and the two reasons for these trends, were considered before projecting the demand parameter to 1990 and 1995. The projections on the bottom line of table 6.1 should be viewed as one scenario based on this information. The forecasts for FIRE employment are multiplied by the demand parameter to obtain forecasts of occupied square footage: line 3 for 1990 and 1995 is line 5 times line 6. Forecasted absorption (at an annual rate) is simply the change in occupied square footage. Note that the annual absorption forecast in table 6.1 is somewhat higher than historical experience. This follows from the assumption about growth in the demand parameter and from projected growth in employment. Alternative estimates reflecting more conservative assumptions need to be made.

Sensitivity of This Method to Assumptions

To illustrate sensitivity analysis, I used the slow growth of the employment ratio: for 1978–81 and 1984–85, the average annual growth in the ratio was 2.9 per year. Table 6.2 shows much-lower absorption forecasts than table 6.1 (620 per year, as opposed to 1,081

Table 6.3 RELIABILITY ANALYSIS: USES 1983 INFORMATION FOR 1985
FORECAST (SQUARE FOOTAGE [IN THOUSANDS]/EMPLOYEE RATIO GROWS
8 PER YEAR)

	Actual 1983	Forecast 1985	Actual 1985	Error 85 (Diff. 1985)
Occupied square footage	9,817.4	11,347.0	12,180.0	(833.0)
Absorption (annual)	1,029.5	764.8	1,113.2	(348.4)
Employment index (FIRE)	67.2	70.0	69.0	1.0
Occupied square footage/ employment index	146.1	162.1	176.5	(14.4)

Note: See description of reliability analysis in the text.

per year). To test the reliability of this method, I used actual data
available in 1983 to forecast to 1985. A forecast of FIRE employment
made in 1982 by the DOL, was used, which showed FIRE employment
growing at an average annual rate of 2 percent, to 70,000 in 1985.

Table 6.3 shows that the employment ratio grew much more rapidly after 1981 than before. This change in trend was captured using
the 1980–83 growth of 8 per year. Thus, the demand parameter was
estimated at 162.1 [equals 146.1 + (2 × 8)] for 1985. Multiplying
line 6 times line 5 in table 6.3 for 1985 gives a forecast of 11,347
square feet of occupied space. This method forecasts absorption of
762 square feet per year as opposed to actual absorption of 1,113
square feet per year (table 6.3). Thus, we have a conservative estimate,
a scenario that protects investors, lenders, and developers.

The Birch Model

David Birch (1986) projected demand for office space over a 10-year
period for each of 249 areas (mostly metropolitan areas) in the United
States. The basis for these projections is estimates of growth in
employment for each industry (e.g., banking, other finance, legal
services, etc.). The following is a simplified version of the Birch
model.

The projections by industry are based on a detailed database on
the number of establishments (a separate location for employment)
in each industry. Birch (1986) has shown that small establishments
are more likely to grow, and by larger percentage amounts, than large
establishments. Furthermore, new (or younger) establishments are
more likely to grow. Therefore, his data on size and age of each
establishment were used as input for his forecast. The type of data

Table 6.4 EXAMPLE OF DEMAND PARAMETERS TRANSLATING OFFICE
EMPLOYMENT INTO SQUARE FOOTAGE PER EMPLOYEE

	Distribution of Occupations							Square Footage Employee
	Manuf.[a]	TCU[b]	Banking[c]	Other Fin.[d]	Legal[e]	Serv.[f]	Gov.[g]	
Managerial	.5	.3	.2	.2	.1	.2	.2	250
Professional	.1	.1	.1	.1	.7	.1	.1	375
Technical	.1	.3	.1	.1	.1	.1	.1	250
Clerical	.2	.2	.5	.5	.1	.5	.5	200

Weighted Average Office Space Needs per Worker						
Manuf.	TCU	Banking	Other Fin.	Legal	Serv.	Gov.
228	228	213	213	333	213	213

Note: Numbers are for illustrative purposes. Percentages (in decimal terms) may not
add to one because of miscellaneous employees who do not occupy additional space.
a. Manuf., office employment in the manufacturing industry, provided that the office
is separate from manufacturing facilities.
b. TCU, separate office establishments in the transportation, communications, and
utilities industries.
c. Banking, employment in the banking industry.
d. Other Fin., employment in other financial activities (stock brokersage, real estate
brokerage, credit unions, etc.).
e. Legal, employment in the legal industry.
f. Serv., office employment in the business services sector (e.g., accounting, secretarial,
delivery, etc.).
g. Gov., employment in the government sector (local, state and national).

used by Birch are generally available from local rental agents, who
keep an inventory of each office tenant classified by industry.
Although agents may not have recorded the number of years the
tenant has been at that location, they can identify tenants who have
leased their space relatively recently.

The next major step in the Birch method translates projections
on industry employment into occupations. The major office-using
occupations (managerial, technical, professional, and clerical) are
unevenly spread across industries, and each occupation has its own
usage of office space.[3] For example, suppose a growth of 1,000 jobs
is projected in banking; of these, 500 are clerical, 100 are technical,
200 are managerial, and 100 are professional.[4] Furthermore, assume
the average square footage consumed per worker indicated in
table 6.4. The square footage per worker is then multiplied by the
number of workers by occupation to find the total square footage
demanded by the banking sector.

Using Industry-by-Occupation Data to Find Square Footage per Worker

The industry-by-occupation breakdown (e.g., 20 percent of banking jobs are managerial) is available (for the whole country as well as by region and state) from the U.S. Department of Commerce, Bureau of Economic Analysis. Table 6.4 transforms this type of information to indicate a percentage distribution of office occupations (managerial, professional, technical, and clerical) for each industry that uses a significant amount of office employment.[5]

Table 6.4 shows how a demand parameter, average office space per worker, can be used with information from an industry by occupation table. The average office space per worker in each occupation, the last column of the table, depends on local market conditions. It is available from local rental agents, appraisers, and property managers.

As an example, consider manufacturing. Table 6.4 assumes that the office employment in this industry is 50 percent managerial, 10 percent professional, 10 percent technical, and 20 percent clerical.[6] These percentages (in decimal terms) are multiplied by the average office space per worker for each occupation (last column in the table). The result, the last row of table 6.4, is the average use of office space by office workers in the manufacturing industry: 228 square feet per worker. Similar calculations for other industries show that business services and government use the lowest amount of office space for an average worker, whereas legal services use the highest amount.

Ragas, Ryan, and Grissom (1992) used surveys of individual tenants to estimate square footage per employee by type of office tenant in New Orleans and Houston. They took pains to be consistent in the definition of square footage used: they favored net rentable area plus a pro rata share of common areas. They found that square footage per employee is considerably lower in the suburbs than downtown, and lower in class-*B* and class-*C* space than in class-*A* space. Also, space per employee is lower in New Orleans than in Houston. These differences appear to be driven primarily by the type of office workers; executives occupy considerably more space than clerical workers. This is confirmed by industry analysis, with law firms having considerably more space per worker than average and travel agencies having considerably less space per worker than average.

Ragas et al. (1992) used regression analysis to verify these conclusions. Furthermore, regression reveals that type of worker and class of space are more important determinants of square footage per employee than rent. An increase in rent did reduce square footage per employee significantly, but a 10 percent increase in rent caused only a 5 percent reduction in square footage per employee in their sample.

Checking Estimates of Square Footage per Worker

Table 6.5 begins with actual data on employment by industry for 1990. Average office space needed per worker, the last row of table 6.4, is multiplied by the number of workers for 1990. This gives total office space needs in each industry. Summing over industries yields an estimate of the total office space occupied in 1990. This number can be checked against total occupied office space in the area as measured by surveys. In this case, rental agents estimated that about 11 million square feet of office space were occupied at the end of 1990. Thus, the estimate from the industry-by-occupation method appears to agree with the survey information obtained by rental agents.

What would the analyst do if the estimated occupied office space in 1990 did not check with independent surveys of occupancy? The first step would be to check the average square footage per employee by occupation in table 6.4. There may be reasons why these numbers have to be adjusted for specific local circumstances. For example, the local industry may be heavily computer intensive, causing larger square footages per employee than in other areas. Or, local banking operations may serve as regional headquarters, causing a greater percentage of managerial employees than other areas. If so, the percentage distribution typical for the banking industry will have to be adjusted for the local area.

Suppose that all the numbers in table 6.4 have been checked and found to be reasonably accurate for the local area, but there is still a discrepancy between the estimated occupied square footage and actual observed occupied square footage. In this case, a reasonable correction would be to adjust all of the weighted average square footages at the bottom of table 6.4. For example, if estimated square footage were 10 percent below actual, then the weighted average square footages could be adjusted upward 10 percent for each industry. This procedure would create complete agreement between estimated and actual occupied square footage.

Forecasting with the Birch Model

The method for forecasting office space demand in 1995 and 2000 is identical to the one used to estimate actual 1990 demand. The

Table 6.5 FORECASTS OF JOBS BY OCCUPATION, OFFICE SPACE NEEDS, CHANGE IN OFFICE SPACE DEMAND, AND ABSORPTION

Year	Manuf.	TCU	Banking	Other Fin.	Legal	Serv.	Gov.	Total
			Forecast of Office Jobs by Type of Business					
1990[a]	4,000	2,000	15,000	4,000	1,000	20,000	5,000	51,000
1995	3,500	2,100	17,000	4,500	1,100	22,000	5,100	55,300
2000	3,300	2,200	19,000	5,000	1,200	24,000	5,200	59,900

Year	Manuf.	TCU	Banking	Other Fin.	Legal	Serv.	Gov.	Total
			Estimated Office Space Needs per Year					
1990[a]	910,000	455,000	3,187,500	850,000	332,500	4,250,000	1,062,500	11,047,500
1995	796,000	477,750	3,612,500	956,250	365,750	4,675,000	1,083,750	11,967,250
2000	750,000	500,500	4,037,500	1,062,500	399,000	5,100,000	1,105,000	12,955,250

Year	Manuf.	TCU	Banking	Other Fin.	Legal	Serv.	Gov.	Total
			Forecast of Change in Office Space Demand (Absorption)					
1990–95	(113,750)	22,750	425,000	106,250	33,250	425,000	21,250	919,750
1995–2000	(45,500)	22,750	425,000	106,250	33,250	425,000	21,250	988,000

Year	Manuf.	TCU	Banking	Other Fin.	Legal	Serv.	Gov.	Total	Percent Total
			Forecast of Absorption per Year						
1990–95	(22,750)	4,550	85,000	21,250	6,650	85,000	4,250	183,950	1.67%
1995–2000	(9,100)	4,550	85,000	21,250	6,650	85,000	4,250	197,600	1.65%

Note: For translation of occupations in table, see notes to table 6.4.
a. Actual data.

weighted average space per employee in a given industry is multiplied by the number of employees forecast in that industry. Total office space demand is the sum of the demand by industry. For example, the 1995 forecasts for the manufacturing industry are based on 3,500 office jobs times 228 square feet per worker, for a total of about 796,000 occupied square feet.[7] Thus, an estimate is provided of total occupied square feet by industry, and of the total summed over all office-using industries. These are important measures of the demand for office space.

This forecast assumes that space per worker is constant. Variables determining space demand per worker were mentioned earlier in this chapter in the discussion of absorption. Rosen, in his essay at the end of this book, includes an interesting analysis of factors determining square footage per employee. He judges that constant space per worker is a reasonable assumption over the decade from 1990 to 2000, and points out that a downward adjustment might be needed if 1990 is used to estimate space per office worker.

Absorption is simply the change in demand for occupied square footage. Thus, the five-year absorption in a given industry can be calculated by finding the change in space demand over the period. Annual absorption (the last two lines of table 6.5) is the five-year absorption divided by five. Finally, absorption of square footage can be converted to a percentage absorption rate by dividing the forecast of absorption by the total occupied square footage at the beginning of the period. For example, 183,950 was divided by 11,047,500 to obtain an average annual absorption rate of 1.67 percent over the 1990–95 period (see table 6.5).

Ragas, Rogers, and Hysom (1991) have pointed out that judgment is required for an office market forecast. In any forecast, it is necessary to distinguish various building types (class A, B or C), but it is often difficult to get data that adequately distinguish among the types. Also, square footage per employee is hard to estimate. One approach is to collect data on office employment and office space in a given area. However, one must ensure that the employment is occupying the relevant space (e.g., class-A space in multitenant buildings within the market area). Alternatively, one can conduct surveys of office tenants to find out how many employees they have and how much space they are occupying. But even here, one must be careful with the definition of occupied space. Tenants occupying a whole floor might define space as gross building area on that floor, whereas tenants occupying part of a floor might define area as net rentable space. More typically, tenants define occupied space to include some share of common areas.

Simplifying the Clapp and Birch Approaches

A simple alternative to the Clapp (1989) and Birch (1986) approaches is to trend recent rates of absorption in the local market. This is standard industry practice where the most recent absorption rate (usually for the previous year) is projected for the following year. For example, if 500,000 square feet of office space were absorbed in the most recent year, then this rate is expected to continue.

Another substitute for the Birch (1986) approach would be to project trends in total employment by industry.[8] Kelly (1983) used government data on employment trends by industry to project office demand growth. In a reasonably stable environment, this method produces good estimates; inaccurate projections occur when industry growth rates change significantly.

Comparing the Clapp and Birch Models

The Birch (1986) model is much more elaborate than the Clapp (1989) approach. For example, it requires data on the actual number of office workers in the office area *by industry*, whereas Clapp uses an index of office workers in the area (all FIRE workers in a broad geographical area in the example given here). In addition, Birch uses square footage per employee *by industry*. These data generally come from surveys requiring that considerable attention be given to the way in which square footage and employees are measured. Clapp simply divides total occupied square footage in the local market by the index of office employment. The only requirement here is that both occupied square footage and employment be measured on a consistent basis over the time interval used for the analysis.

Does the greater complexity of the Birch (1986) approach produce more accurate forecasts? It likely does. For example, the Birch approach allows one to check total occupied square footage derived from surveys of number of workers and of space per worker by industry against total occupied square footage estimated by real estate appraisers and brokers. This check on accuracy is not available with the Clapp (1989) approach. On the other hand, the Birch approach is clearly more costly and time consuming to implement than the

Clapp approach. Is the extra cost justified by improved forecasts? This question must be evaluated with empirical studies. I know of no studies of this issue to date.

FORECASTING THE SUPPLY SIDE

Birch (1986) simply trended growth in the total supply of office space, producing a "what if" scenario. Thus, for each metropolitan area, he calculated growth in office space from 1975 to 1985. Then he asked what the consequences would be for the vacancy rate if total space grew by the same amount over the subsequent decade (1985 through 1995).

Over a three-to-five-year period, reasonable supply projections can be made by examining office space that is proposed (in the planning stage, or a permit obtained) or under construction. Even if no new construction projects are begun, this "pipeline" of projects that are under way can be reasonably predicted to add to the existing supply of space. Since it takes a long time to plan and build office space, this method is very accurate over short time periods (one to two years) and fairly accurate over intermediate time periods (three to five years).

Data sources on proposed and under-construction properties include a "windshield survey" of under-construction property and a review of construction permits granted by the local government. Zoning applications, newspaper stories, and word-of-mouth rumors can supplement these data sources.

Figure 6.2 depicts the flow of new space as a river that begins with a developer's idea, followed by the purchase of land or an option to purchase land. Analysis of the proposed project then begins. If the project appears economically and financially feasible, an application for approval by planning and zoning is filed. This, together with construction permits, is often the first formal public announcement of the project. Once construction begins, the project becomes obvious to a "windshield survey" of the area. The whole process, from idea to completion, typically takes one to five years or more.

After the public authorities have finished their final inspection of new space, a certificate of occupancy (CO) is issued. At this point, the new space enters the "pool" of vacant space available for lease

Figure 6.2 CONSTRUCTION AND RENTAL OF MULTITENANT OFFICE SPACE

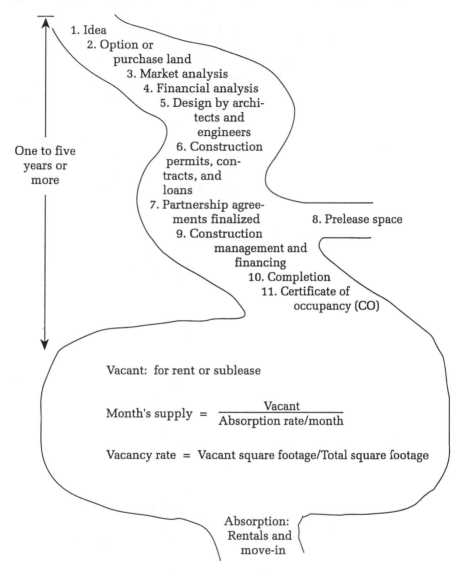

or sublease. Then the space may be absorbed by the market (i.e., occupied by tenants), leaving the pool of vacant space. As pointed out earlier in this chapter, the rental of new space is taken as approximately equivalent to absorption.[9]

Forecasting Rents, Expenses, and Net Operating Income

There are two major influences on rents and expenses that are somewhat predictable. The first is inflation. As indicated in chapter 1, rents and expenses generally tend to grow with inflation. To the extent that inflation is predictable (e.g., by a consensus of economists at the national level), then office rents and expenses are somewhat predictable.

Real rents and expenses can be obtained by dividing actual rents and expenses by the consumer price index (CPI). Real rents and expenses are somewhat predictable from analysis of the business cycle. Recall that real rents respond to the difference between actual vacancy rates and natural vacancy rates (chapter 3). After considering the lags involved, real rents tend to rise when the natural vacancy rate is above the actual vacancy rate and to fall when the actual vacancy rate is relatively high.

Real expenses tend to be less responsive to the business cycle than rents. Therefore, when rents are rising strongly in real terms, the ratio of expenses to rents tends to fall. This causes net operating income to rise in real terms. Conversely, when real rents are falling, expenses don't fall as much. Net operating income is squeezed when the office market is in the downward part of the cycle.

Forecasting is facilitated by working with real rents and expenses: real dollar values can be forecasted separately from inflation. This is important because very different methodologies are used for the two forecasts. For example, inflation might be forecasted from a weighted average of past rates of inflation or by manipulating changes in the money supply. For many real estate purposes, inflation would be forecasted by a consensus forecast from business economists.[10]

Forecasts for inflation can be combined with forecasts for real dollar values to produce forecasts of the nominal dollar values of rents and expenses. For example, if inflation is expected to be 10 percent over a three-year horizon and real growth is expected to be 10 percent over the same horizon, then the nominal dollar values can be expected to grow by 21 percent (equals 10 percent + 10 percent + 10 × 10 percent).

McIntosh and Henderson (1989) examined the efficient-markets hypothesis (EMH) as applied to the office market. Specifically, they tested the hypothesis that past returns on office buildings can be used to project future returns.[11] Based on monthly data from 127 office transactions from January 1979 through January 1985 in the Dallas–Fort Worth area, they found that returns in one month were significantly related to returns in the previous month, but that the relationships do not have much forecasting power. They concluded that "the serial correlation present in office property in the Dallas-Fort Worth market is not enough to enable an investor to consistently earn abnormal return using past price information" (p. 67).

Vacancy Projections

Once projections are made on demand and supply, it is straightforward to project changes in vacancy. For example, if absorption is expected to be 500,000 square feet and new supply is expected to be 700,000 square feet, both in the next year, then vacancy can be projected to increase by 200,000 square feet. This figure is added to the current vacant space and divided by the projected stock of office space (the current stock plus the 700,000 addition) to get a projected vacancy rate.

Examples: Applications of Models

Ragas et al. (1991) implemented a model similar to the Birch (1986) approach to demand and supply. They used data from the U.S. Census to estimate the percentage of office employment in each industry. These percentages were combined with forecasts on total employment by industry in New Orleans to forecast office workers. Finally, they used an estimate of square footage per employee in New Orleans to translate estimated growth in office workers into absorption of new space.

Their estimates of the percentage of office workers by industry in New Orleans during 1985–90 were as follows:

	Office Workers (%)
Manufacturing	6
Mining	81
Construction	4
Transportation, utilities	8
Wholesale trade	2
Retail trade	5
Finance, insurance, and real estate	100
Services	42
Government	30

Generally, these figures corroborate other estimates. However, the percentage for mining appears to be much higher than normal, perhaps because of special characteristics of the city of New Orleans. Also, the percentage for government is low because the authors excluded government employees working in space owned by the government; this space is not competitive with the rest of the office market.

Price Waterhouse (1992) applied these methods to downtown Los Angeles office markets. Under-construction properties were used to project the growth of supply. Employment growth and the usage of office space by different types of workers were used to project demand. Price Waterhouse found it helpful to distinguish "premier" office buildings (sometimes termed "trophy" buildings) from the rest of the office stock. They reported a 12 percent vacancy rate in premier buildings after a 24-month absorption period, whereas both class-B and class-C buildings had a 32 percent vacancy rate. They pointed out that these are gross vacancies; that is, they include space available for sublease. They concluded that overbuilding has kept vacancy rates high and rents on new space very low by historical standards.

LOCATION DECISIONS AND OFFICE DYNAMICS

A location or relocation decision may be associated with a decision about expansion or contraction of office employment. For example, a change in telecommunications technology may alter the cost-effective location for clerical and administrative support staff, allowing them to move to lower-rent facilities while still maintaining adequate contact with headquarters. At the same time, the new technology may make their activities more efficient. In this example, the relocation decision is associated with a contraction in employment and a reduction in wages and office rents (since these costs are generally lower in more remote locations).

Clapp, Pollakowski, and Lynford (1992) integrated the location decision with a standard neoclassical dynamic model. They used a variety of data sources to investigate submarkets in the Boston metropolitan area with annual data from 1980 to 1989. Their framework captures an important dichotomy between central city and suburban office markets: central cities have much-slower growth in occupied space but faster growth in FIRE employment. The central city also contains relatively large concentrations of faster-growing sectors such as business and legal services. Clapp and colleagues' (1992) empirical results show that agglomerations by type of office employment do influence demand growth. Areas concentrating in industries typically growing rapidly generally experience faster demand growth. Thus, achieving a concentration of successful industries breeds further success.

Implications of Contact Patterns for Office Vacancy

Structural changes at the national, regional, and local levels have long-term implications for office vacancy rates. The contact patterns literature provides a useful perspective on 5- to 10-year changes in office vacancy rates at all levels of spatial aggregation. There are two aspects to the theoretical structure needed for these forecasts. First, rents are slow to adjust, and the supply of space is even slower (see discussion of the natural vacancy rate). Changes in vacancy follow from comparing expected growth in demand to lagged growth in supply.

A second part of the theory originates in the economic base model, which says that employment is particularly important in industries that export their goods or services outside the local area. By selling their products elsewhere, these industries bring money into the local area. Some of this money is spent on goods and services produced locally, creating further income and jobs. Thus, growth or decline in these basic (exporting) industries has a multidimensional impact on the local economy. Recall Marshall's (1983) contention that independent establishments or regional headquarters are more likely to buy business services locally than branches of major corporations. Thus, these types of exporting activities have a bigger impact on the local economy.

This implies that growth in independent establishments or regional headquarters will have strong positive consequences for office demand in the local and regional office markets.[12] Using data for Washington State, Beyers and Alvine (1985) showed that small-business service firms export a surprisingly large percentage of their services (see discussion in chapter 4). Thus, small firms may contribute as much, or more, to growth in basic employment as large firms. Sectors particularly helpful to growth in demand include computer services, research and development laboratories, management consulting, architecture, and engineering. Schmenner (1991) found similar evidence for four midwestern states. Thus, areas that can expect growth in these types of business services can also expect a more positive outlook for office demand, and, therefore, for office vacancy rates.

Suburbanization is another important demand-side factor. Clerical and administrative support employment ("back-office" activities) are suburbanizing at a much faster rate than other types of office activity. The contact patterns literature explains this by improvements in telecommunications that allow activities with relatively routine contact patterns to move to more remote locations (Daniels 1979).

This implies that areas with heavy concentrations of back-office employment should experience more rapid suburbanizing trends. In general, that demand growth has been much more rapid in the suburbs: For example, in the Boston area the three suburban counties (Essex, Middlesex, and Norfolk) had office employment growing at an average annual rate of 7 percent, whereas the Boston downtown (Suffolk County) had a 4.7 percent average annual growth rate (Clapp et al. 1992). How, then, does one explain vacancy rates in the suburbs that average 3–7 percent greater than in the downtown?[13] A possible answer is that higher demand growth has caused the natural vacancy rate to be higher in the suburbs than in the downtown.[14]

Risk Analysis

This chapter has emphasized projecting future demand, supply, vacancy rate, expenses, and rents. As stated at the outset, it is necessary to try to project the long-term future because real estate development and investment decisions are long-term commitments. Yet, forecasting is hazardous because no one knows what the future will be. The best we can hope to do is to determine the broad outlines of future changes in demand and supply.

Given that any forecast of the future is subject to considerable error, one must allow for a range of possible future outcomes. The analyst can use detailed knowledge of demand and supply conditions to make reasonable estimates of optimistic and pessimistic scenarios on future demand and supply. When creating such scenarios, the extremes of the range are not of great interest. For example, an extremely pessimistic scenario would allow for global war and economic collapse, a possible, but not very probable, outcome. Therefore, it is better to strive for reasonably pessimistic and reasonably optimistic scenarios.[15] It is important, then, to translate the optimistic, most likely, and pessimistic range of outcomes into hard numbers useful for investment, development, and public policy. The next chapter gives an example of how this can be done.

CONCLUSIONS

Since no one can know the future, the most sensible course is to make a conservative estimate, solidly grounded in current realities. A probable future scenario holds that absorption will be closely linked to employment change. Figure 6.1 illustrates how projections and forecasts on employment growth can be used with demand parameters to produce absorption estimates.

Some simple steps are required to use the model proposed here:

1. Define demand segments, such as employment in financial institutions, for the property being analyzed;
2. Obtain third-party forecasts for the growth of employment in the local area in each demand segment;
3. Evaluate those forecasts and change them if necessary;
4. Find information on square footage of occupied office space;
5. Use spreadsheet software to generate demand parameters—numbers relating employment to the amount of office space demanded (table 6.1);
6. Use the employment or population forecasts and demand parameters to forecast absorption;
7. Conduct sensitivity analysis to evaluate the downside risk (i.e., risk that absorption will be lower than expected) (tables 6.2 and 6.3).

The Birch (1986) model is driven by employment projections by industry. Although this is a complex method for projecting employment growth, simple extrapolations can be used. Alternatively, state and federal agencies can furnish growth forecasts in employment by industry. Birch uses employment forecasts to estimate absorption of office space by industry. His methodology depends on using information on the number of employees in each occupation for each industry. These data are combined with information on the square footage per employee by occupation (tables 6.4, 6.5).

There is another piece to the story: future growth in the supply of space will have some impact on absorption. If supply growth is relatively slow, vacancy rates can become low (e.g., near zero). In this case, limited supply constrains the growth in demand. On the other hand, rapid growth in supply will cause easy market conditions (high vacancy and discounted market rents). This can increase absorption. Thus, the supply side, as indicated by proposed or under-construction space, can be evaluated as an extension of the analysis proposed here.

Supply can be forecast from the flow of new construction: from the idea's inception through the planning and permitting process to the completion of construction and issuance of a certificate of occupancy (figure 6.2). Since this process takes two to five years for office properties, supply is predictable over most of this time period.

Rents, expenses, and net operating income are difficult to forecast. However, some forecastability can be obtained by dividing these dollar values into real (i.e., inflation-adjusted) dollars and an inflation component. Inflation is imperfectly forecastable by business economists. The real component of rents responds to the cycle of office demand, construction, and vacancy. Growth in real expenses can be extrapolated into the future. Finally, expected inflation can be added to expected growth in real dollar values to obtain forecasts on rents, expenses, and NOI.

The contact patterns literature (see chapter 5) has made some important contributions to long-range forecasting. Structural changes in transportation and telecommunication cause long-term shifts in office employment and construction of office space. An obvious example of this is improved transmission of computer data, access to desk-top terminals, and facsimile transmission of documents. All of these changes have allowed routine operations such as computing, bookkeeping, and secretarial activities to shift from the center of the city toward less-expensive suburban or small-town locations. Related trends have created a market where the demand for suburban office space is largely from smaller, less-credit-worthy tenants.

The contact patterns literature has also examined linkages between office firms and the rest of the local economy. Independent office establishments (not branch offices) have a greater demand for services from other local businesses. For example, they may demand legal, financial, accounting, or advertising services. Thus, a community that is successful in attracting these independent establishments has a greater potential for growth than one that attracts branch offices. Ihlanfeldt and Raper (1990) and Raper and Ihlanfeldt (at the end of this volume) provide convincing evidence for this.

Clapp and colleagues (1992) have established a connection between the dynamic path of office absorption and spatial patterns of office locations. Because of agglomeration economies, submarkets that establish nodes of rapidly growing office industries are likely to benefit from further growth in the future. Conversely, those towns specializing in industries with slow growth are likely to have difficulty attracting high-growth office activities.

Notes

1. The early stages of the effect of a soft market on absorption and collateral value were documented by Goldman-Sachs (1986).

2. This decline was pointed out to me by Hank Wise of Pritchett, Ball and White, of Atlanta. He also commented that absorption can be a function of short-term market interest rates (e.g., the prime rate).

3. Birch (1986) included sales occupations, but these are generally not considered to be office-using occupations.

4. The numbers of workers by occupation add up to 900. The remaining 100 office workers do *not* occupy additional space because they share space or work in areas allocated to machines. For example, part-time workers share space and other workers perform jobs as messengers, security personnel, or copy-room clerks. In a sense these workers are squeezed into the space allocated to other workers and to machines.

5. The numbers used here are for illustrative purposes only.

6. These numbers do not add to 100 percent because some workers do not use additional space. For example, several part-time workers share one carrel.

7. The square feet per employee numbers in table 6.4 are rounded (in this case, there are about 227.5 square feet) and the total square feet in table 6.5 are rounded off, so a calculator will produce slightly different numbers for the total in table 6.5.

8. In Connecticut, the Department of Labor projects these trends for subareas within the state.

9. This is an approximation, because those renting space may decide to sublease all or part of it. If so, the rented space returns to the pool of available space. Also, one needs to make sure that the tenants have not vacated other space in the same market.

10. Economists often forecast inflation by using sophisticated statistical methods for extracting inflationary expectations from interest rates on long-term bonds.

11. Returns can be defined as appreciation in value plus net operating income (NOI) as a percentage of beginning value.

12. This assumes, of course, that there is an adequate supply of typing services, employment agencies, and other local services to attract and support the types of offices that export their services.

13. The 3–7 percent figure is for the seven years, 1984–91, that Coldwell Banker has been keeping data aggregated over all of the cities in their database.

14. Of course, suburban vacancy rates in many areas became too high by 1990 because supply had grown too fast relative to the shift to the suburbs. Thus, the key to applied analysis is to compare projected demands to projected supply to evaluate actual vacancy rate relative to the natural rate.

15. A reasonably optimistic (pessimistic) scenario can be conceptualized as one with a 25 percent probability of a better (worse) outcome.

Chapter Seven

APPLICATIONS TO OFFICE INVESTMENTS: A CASE STUDY

This chapter integrates the theory and empirical results discussed in previous chapters with the actual decisions of lenders, appraisers, developers, investors, local public policy officials, and other real estate professionals. More specifically, tools developed earlier in this volume are used to construct forecasts and plausible scenarios of the most important variables that determine the success or failure of an office project. For example, estimates of the natural vacancy rate, changes in the actual vacancy rate, rent, changes in rent, absorption time (i.e., rent-up period), costs, growth in costs, and related variables can be incorporated into a model with implications for decisions made by real estate professionals.

The most important decision variables used by real estate professionals include an income statement, net operating income, revenues, expenses, net cash flows, borrowing needs, mortgage payments, resale values, and present values of future cash flows. A model that ties the knot between these decision variables and market analysis must consider lease rollover, fit-up costs, leasing expenses, taxes, and the terms of borrowing. This chapter produces a model of this type.

USES OF THE MODEL

Potential applications of such a model include:

1. Mortgage analysis: determination of borrowing needs and implications of these needs for cash flows and net present values;
2. Lease analysis: choosing between short and long leases, given various assumptions on fit-up costs, leasing commissions, and future rental rates;
3. Risk analysis: market analysis provides alternative assumptions

Figure 7.1 INPUT TABLE FOR MODEL RENT-UP OF OFFICE BUILDING

Lease term (years)	2
Average annual rent per square foot ($)	21
Quarters to stabilized occupancy	14
Stabilized occupancy (%)	85
Net rentable area in square feet	100,000
Percentage preleased	20
Leasing commission (%)	6
Tenant improvement cost per square foot ($)	20
Expenses per square foot occupied ($)	8.20
Expenses per square foot vacant ($)	6.80
Income growth rate (%)	4.5
Expense growth rate (%)	4.5
Discount rate (required return) (%)	15
Resale cap rate (%)	10.5
Mortgage interest rate (%)	9
Cost per square foot ($)	100
Cost of land ($)	2,000,000
Cost of completed project: land + construction ($)	12,000,000
Loan amount ($)	10,000,000
Loan term (years)	15
Commercial or residential (C or R)	C
Tax bracket (local, state, and federal) (%)	40
- -	
Required loan payment ($)	101,426.66
Yearly depreciation ($)	317,460.32

Notes: Assumptions in the model are supported by market analysis. Values below the dashed line are calculated by the model; those above the line are entered by the user (see the text for discussion of the numbers). Stabilized occupancy can be measured by one minus the natural vacancy rate; this is the occupancy rate that can be reasonably expected for a building of a given type in the local market.

that produce optimistic and pessimistic scenarios on cash flows and other decision variables.

The model is introduced here with an example of lease analysis. A case study is then presented as an example of mortgage analysis.

MODEL STRUCTURE

Figure 7.1 displays the information entered into the model. Figure 7.2 provides an example of the calculations performed by the model and defines the terms.[1] A review of these figures provides a good overview of the structure of the model.

It is useful to distinguish between information entered into the model (figure 7.1) as a result of market analysis and additional information required to integrate market analysis and real estate decisions. The most important numbers that come from market analysis are: average annual rent, quarters to stabilize occupancy, the stabilized occupancy rate, percentage preleased, income growth rate, expense growth rate, lease term, and expenses per square foot.[2]

Data for lease term, average annual rent, expenses per square foot, and so on, are derived from analysis of the competition and from industry sources such as the Building Owners and Managers Association (BOMA) of the Institute for Real Estate Management (IREM). Chapter 1 describes rental income and expense figures available from BOMA. The composition of operating expenses and income is defined in detail in BOMA publications and is summarized in the notes to figure 7.2.

Absorption analysis (see chapter 6) is the source of information on the number of quarters to stabilize occupancy (14 quarters in figure 7.1). The level of stabilized occupancy (85 percent occupancy rate in figure 7.1) is derived from the natural vacancy rate (see chapters 2 and 3: stabilized occupancy equals one minus natural vacancy rate for the area).[3] Accurate information of this type is obviously essential for safe and sound lending, and for investment or appraisal decisions. An increase in absorption time (more quarters to stabilize occupancy) means that the receipt of rental income will be delayed. This reduces cash flows available to pay debt and also reduces the value of the project. Likewise, lower stabilized occupancy means more space that is vacant and not earning rent.

Estimated growth rates for rent and expenses are among the inputs in figure 7.1.[4] These growth rates can come from the extrapolation of historical experience, as indicated by the discussion in chapter 1. Alternatively, expense growth can come from forecasts on the rate of inflation, and income growth can be derived from an analysis of the gap between actual vacancy rates and natural vacancy rates (see chapter 3). These numbers must be carefully considered, since they play a vital role in the determination of cash flows and values.

As already indicated, some of the information needed to complete the analysis comes from industry sources such as BOMA, which provide estimates for operating costs per square foot occupied and vacant, and for leasing commissions. The leasing commission used here is a percentage of the total amount of rent due under the terms of the lease. Any renewal by the same tenant pays a commission at the rate of one-half of the percentage paid on the original lease.[5]

Figure 7.2 OUTPUT TABLES FROM THE MODEL

a. Monthly Information

	Year 1, Quarter 1			Year 1, Quarter 2
	Month 1	Month 2	Month 3	Month 4
Occupancy (%)	21.50	23.10	24.64	26.19
Total square feet leased	21,548	23,095	24,643	26,190
New area leased	21,548	1,548	1,548	1,548
Area released				
Rent per square foot ($)	21.00	21.08	21.16	21.24
Effective gross income ($)	37,708	40,427	43,156	45,894
Expenses per square foot occupied ($)	8.20	8.23	8.26	8.29
Expenses per square foot vacant ($)	6.80	6.83	6.85	6.88
Expenses ($)	59,181	59,584	59,989	60,397
Net operating income ($)	(21,472)	(19,157)	(16,834)	(14,502)
Leasing commission ($)	54,300	3,915	3,929	3,944
Tenant improvement cost (work letter) ($)	430,952	30,952	30,952	30,952
Cash flow before debt service ($)	(506,725)	(54,024)	(51,715)	(49,399)
Interest expense on loan ($)	75,000	79,363	80,363	81,354
Payment (principal plus interest) to amortize loan ($)	101,427	107,899	109,555	111,208
Additional financing required ($)	581,725	133,387	132,079	130,753
Loan balance ($)	10,581,725	10,715,111	10,847,190	10,977,943
Taxable income ($)	(122,927)	(124,975)	(123,652)	(122,311)
Taxes due ($)	(49,171)	(49,990)	(49,461)	(48,924)
Resale in year 10				
Aftertax cash flow plus resale ($)	(532,554)	(83,397)	(82,618)	(81,828)
Discounted cash flow plus resale ($)	(525,979)	(81,350)	(79,596)	(77,861)
Cumulative discounted cash flow ($)	(525,979)	(607,329)	(686,925)	(764,786)

b. Annual Summaries

	Year 1	Year 2	Year 3
1. Effective gross income ($)	634,182	1,042,167	2,184,176
2. Expenses ($)	737,263	798,895	864,634
3. Net operating income (1–2) ($)	(103,081)	243,272	1,319,543
4. Initial leasing commission ($)	98,177	49,972	105,971
5. Tenant improvements ($)	771,429	371,429	757,143
6. Cash flow before debt service (3–4–5) ($)	(972,687)	(178,129)	456,429
7. Interest expense on loan ($)	1,001,351	1,133,498	1,243,150
8. Payment (principal plus interest) to amortize loan ($)	1,378,988	1,618,339	1,848,757
9. Additional financing required ($)	1,974,037	1,311,627	786,721
10. Loan balance ($)	11,974,037	13,285,665	14,072,386

Notes: Definitions of terms used in the model follow.

Occupancy: This row gives end-of-month occupancy as a percentage of total space available for the property. It is determined by taking the amount of space preleased and adding to it the amount of space that must be rented each month to achieve the specified stabilized occupancy in the specified time ("quarters to stabilized occupancy," figure 7.1). Note that this assumes that the rentup is linear from the amount of space preleased to the stabilized occupancy level.

The additional space (as a percentage) that is leased each month is given by:

$$\frac{(\text{Stabilized occupancy} - \text{Percentage preleased})}{\text{Months to stabilized occupancy}} \tag{7.1}$$

Additional area is leased each month until the stabilized occupancy figure is reached.

Total square feet leased: This row provides the total square footage that has been leased through the end of the current month. This area is determined by:

$$\text{Occupancy} \times \text{Net rentable area} \tag{7.2}$$

(continued)

Figure 7.2 OUTPUT TABLES FROM THE MODEL (continued)

New area leased (square feet): This row lists only the square footage that is leased during the current month. This area is given by:

$$\frac{(\text{Stabilized occupancy} - \text{Percentage preleased})}{\text{Months to Stabilized Occupancy}} \times \text{Net rentable area} \qquad (7.3)$$

Area released (square feet): This row lists area that has been released. It is assumed that all leased space will be released at the market rent per square foot at the expiration of the previous lease. This does not occur within the first year.

Rent per square foot ($ per year): This row lists the annual rent per square foot that is being charged for space leased in the current month. The initial annual rent per square foot is specified in the input table ("Average annual rent"). Also specified in the input table is the "Income growth rate" (as an annual percentage rate). This value indicates the rate at which the rent per square foot will grow. The annual rent per square foot listed for each month is given by:

$$\text{Rent per Square Foot (previous month)} \times [1 + (\text{Income growth rate}/12)] \qquad (7.4)$$

Effective gross income: This row lists the total estimated monthly income received from the space that has been leased. This value is found by summing the "New area leased" for all previous months times the corresponding annual "Rent per square foot" and dividing by 12 to put the income on a monthly basis.

Expenses per square foot occupied: This row lists the total annual operating expenses incurred for each square foot of leased space. The "Expenses per square foot occupied," given on the input table (figure 7.1), increase each month at the rate specified in the input table for the expense growth rate (given as an annual percentage rate). "Operating expenses" include real estate taxes, property insurance, utilities, materials and labor for cleaning and repairs, management expenses, and reserves for replacements. Operating expenses *do not* include any financing expenses or any expenses related to income taxes. In particular, depreciation is not an operating expense.

Expenses per square foot vacant: This row lists the total annual operating expenses incurred for each square foot of vacant space. The "Expenses per square foot vacant" increase each month at the rate specified in the input table for the expense growth rate (given as an annual percentage rate).

Expenses: This row lists the total monthly operating expenses incurred for both occupied (leased) and vacant space. This value is found by multiplying the "Total square feet leased" by "Expenses per square foot occupied" and adding to this the amount of unoccupied space ("Net rentable area" minus "Total square feet leased") multiplied by the "Expenses per square foot vacant." Divide this sum by 12 to put it on a monthly basis.

Net operating income (NOI): "Effective gross income" minus "Total operating expenses."

Leasing commission: Calculated as the "Leasing commission" percentage times "Lease term" in years times "Rent per square foot" times square footage covered by the lease (all data from figure 7.1). For a lease renewal, the leasing commission is half the original commission.

Tenant improvement (work letter): The landlord is responsible for floor covering, partitions, ceilings, and interior decoration to suit the needs of the tenant. Calculated as the tenant improvement cost per square foot (figure 7.1) times square footage covered by the lease.

Cash flow before debt service: NOI minus "Leasing commission" minus "Tenant improvement cost."

Interest rate and payment: The loan payment is calculated from the given interest rate (figure 7.1) assuming a fixed rate mortgage over the term of the loan given in figure 7.1. If the loan is a variable rate loan, simply use the most-likely interest rate over the term of the loan. Often, this is the initial interest rate, since interest rates will sometimes be higher and sometimes lower.

Additional financing required and Loan balance: If cash flows are less than interest payments, then additional financing is required and the loan balance goes up by the amount of the additional financing. If cash flows are greater than or equal to interest payments, then no additional financing is required and loan balance can go down or remain the same. The maximum payment to the loan is the loan payment that will repay the loan with interest over its term. If there are any additional cash flows beyond this, they become net cash flows to the equity investors.

Taxable income: Taxable income is equal to "Cash flow before debt service" minus "Interest expense" minus "Depreciation expense."

Taxes due: Taxes equal "Taxable income" times "Tax bracket." The examples given here assume that investors can use the tax shelter provided by negative taxable income (e.g., they can reduce taxable income from other real estate projects).

Resale in year 10: The holding period in this model is assumed to be 10 years. Resale in year 10 has a value only for the last month in the 10th year when it is equal to NOI divided by the resale cap rate.

Aftertax cash flow (ATCF) plus resale: This is cash flow to the investor. It is equal to "Cash flow before debt service" minus "Debt service" minus "Taxes due."

Discounted cash flow (DCF): The value in today's dollars (i.e., present value) of the cash flow on the line above. Present value is calculated using the investor's required rate of return.

Cumulative discounted cash flow: The sum of all the discounted cash flows from the first time period through the current time period. At year 10, this line indicates the feasibility of the project: it is not feasible if the cumulative discounted cash flows are less than the cost of the investment.

Other information comes from inspection of the building and knowledge of construction and land costs. Rentable square footages, building type (always commercial [Class C] for office buildings), total construction costs, and total land costs are obtained from these sources. Here, construction costs include soft costs such as construction loan interest, architectural fees, and application costs (e.g., for local permissions), as well as hard costs associated with physical construction.

Finally, each individual (or institutional) investor has specific information that helps to determine the financial success of the project. For example, each investor has his or her unique tax bracket (i.e., the additional federal, state, and local taxes paid on each additional dollar earned). Furthermore, each investor has a unique need to borrow, so the amount of the mortgage loan and the interest paid on the loan will vary from individual to individual. Lastly, the required rate of return is the investor's "hurdle rate," the rate of return that the investor expects to earn on investments of comparable risk.

The cap rate is the "going out" capitalization rate used by appraisers. This rate is divided into the net income from operations at the end of the investor's holding period. In this model, the holding period is set at 10 years. Therefore, whenever net operating income is available at the end of 10 years, it is simply divided by the cap rate to determine the terminal value (i.e., resale value) of the property.

APPLICATIONS OF MODEL TO NEW AND EXISTING BUILDINGS

Figures 7.1 and 7.2 are designed for analysis of a newly constructed office building. The amount of space preleased is assumed to pay rent immediately (i.e., it counts as occupied space). The key to the financial success of this new building depends on the amount preleased, stabilized occupancy and the rate of absorption (quarters to stabilize occupancy), as well as average rent per square foot and operating costs per square foot. Construction costs are used to establish the basis for tax depreciation; the sum of construction costs and land costs is used for net present-value calculations. The model is not designed to deal with costs during the time of construction.

The model is easily adapted to acquisition of an existing office building. In this case, preleased space is equal to the existing occupancy level, and the amount of leasing commission on this space is set to zero. The lease term for this space would be set to the average term of existing leases, where the average is calculated to weight the leases on large amounts of space more heavily than the lease on small amounts of space. In this way, lease renewal at the market rate would approximate the average experience of the building.

To perform an accurate tax analysis for an existing building, it is necessary to set construction costs per square foot at a level that gives the correct depreciable basis of the building. For example, if the existing building has a depreciable basis of $10 million and 100,000 square feet of rental space, then construction costs should equal $100 per square foot, as in figure 7.1. If the total acquisition costs of the existing building were $13 million, then land costs would be set to $3 million to get accurate net present-value calculations.

LEASE TERM ANALYSIS

Figure 7.2 gives the first few years of data for a two-year lease term. This is an exceptionally short term for an office lease. In fact, the average term of office leases has decreased from 10–15 years in the 1970s to about 5 years today. The model can be used to change the lease term to see what term is most beneficial financially. A shorter lease term has higher risk of vacancy and higher leasing commissions, but it allows the landlord to benefit from increases in market rental rates. Longer lease terms give the landlord more predictability of cash flows as well as some protection against declines in market rental rates.

Figure 7.2 shows that the occupancy rate increases at about 1.5 percent per month as the building moves from 20 percent occupancy (preleased) to 85 percent stabilized occupancy in 42 months: 85 percent − 20 percent = 65 percent ÷ 42 months = 1.5 percent. The average amount of space leased over the 14 quarters (42 months) is 1,548 square feet per month. The total square footage leased (second row, figure 7.2) is as of the end of the month.

Rents and expenses per square foot increase at the 4.5 percent annual rate given in figure 7.1. That is, the average increase in rents is projected to be about 8¢ per month, whereas the increase in expenses is projected to be about 3¢ per month. Effective gross income (EGI), expenses, and net operating income (NOI) are calculated following the method given in the notes to figure 7.2.

Figure 7.3 COMPARISON OF TWO-YEAR AND FIVE-YEAR LEASES

	Lease Term	
	Two-Year	Five-Year
Net operating income becomes positive	yr. 1, mo. 11	yr. 1, mo. 10
Net cash flow becomes positive[a]	yr. 5, mo. 3	yr. 3, mo. 3
Additional financing no longer required	yr. 5, mo. 2	yr. 6, mo. 2
Maximum loan balance ($)	14,072,000	15,747,000
Present value of all future cash flows ($)[a]	11,251,894	5,492,188

Notes: Stabilized occupancy is 88 percent for the five-year leases and 85 percent for the two-year leases. Other assumptions are given in figure 7.1.
a. Cash flows are after tax and net of financing expenses.

Expenses associated with leasing dominate the absorption period (i.e., the period before stabilized occupancy is achieved). An important part of these expenses is tenant improvements (TI, sometimes referred to as "work letter"). These occur when the landlord finishes interior space with partitions, carpeting, wall covering, and related materials. Tenant improvements are the subject of intense negotiations between landlords and tenants and are often major expenses for landlords.

Because of the heavy expenses associated with leasing and tenant improvements, net cash flows are projected to be negative during the first two years of the building's operation (see the annual summary, part *b*, figure 7.2). This causes the loan balance to increase because cash flows are insufficient to pay interest on the loan. The model uses an increase in loan balance to demonstrate that additional cash is needed. The loan is one such source; alternately, equity capital could be used to offset the negative cash flows. The point is that some source of additional capital will be needed for a considerable time period. Furthermore, the suppliers of that capital will require a fair rate of return on their funds.

Figure 7.3 compares two-year leases to five-year leases. Since we expect lower average vacancy rates with the five-year leases, stabilized occupancy has been raised to 88 percent for the five-year leases, whereas it remains at 85 percent for the two-year leases; all other assumptions in figure 7.1 are retained.

As can be seen from figure 7.3, the two-year leases generally are expected to perform better than the five-year leases. The former have lower maximum loan balance and higher present value of future cash flows. On the other hand, they have substantially longer projected negative cash flows. The reason for longer negative cash flows is higher tenant improvements in years three through five, when the two leases come up for renewal: the two-year leases have about $750,000 of tenant improvements in year three, as opposed to $389,000 for the five-year leases.

The superior performance of two-year leases occurs because of rising rental rates. In year three, the preleased space is renewed and all of the space leased during year one is released during year three. At the end of year three, all of the space released during that year is projected to earn higher rents than under the five-year leases. Thus, effective gross income is projected to be about $2,184,000 in year three with the two-year leases, as opposed to $1,517,000 under the five-year leases. After year three, the average rental rate under two-year leases is always higher than under five-year leases, so the five-year leases never catch up with the two-year leases.

The analysis shows that the lower vacancy rate associated with the five-year leases is not sufficient to counterbalance the lower average rental rate. Therefore, the two-year leases have higher present value of cash flows and lower total lending requirements. Of course, the five-year leases would do better in a situation where market rental rates were falling, provided all other assumptions were similar to those in figure 7.3.

CASE STUDY OF SOMERSET ASSOCIATES: FALL 1990

Somerset Associates (SA), of Stamford, Conn., is a limited partnership that owns one asset: a small (24,887 square feet) class-A, multi-tenant, general purpose, office building in Stamford. The building was constructed in 1980. It is currently 29.5 percent vacant; the remaining 17,553 square feet are rented at an average rent of $2.42 per square foot per month. Operating expenses are about $.90 per month per leasable square foot (vacant and occupied). The mortgage balance owed to First Bank is $4 million, with the interest rate to be determined by Chapter 11 bankruptcy proceedings.

Somerset Associates was formed in 1986 with the sole purpose of acquiring the Somerset Avenue building. After expending $1,200,000 in organizational fees, a little over $5,000,000 was used to acquire the building. In 1990 the building was appraised at between $2 and $3 million and in 1991 bank officials estimated they could net between $2 million and $2.5 million from the sale of the property.

The issue in the Chapter 11 bankruptcy proceedings is sometimes referred to as "cram-down analysis." A cram down is successful if the loan is reconstructed to reduce interest and/or to allow unpaid interest to be added to the loan balance until the property provides sufficient cash flow to pay full interest on the accumulated amount of the loan. The borrower retains an ownership interest subject to supervision by the court. The borrower can charge a reasonable fee for management of the property, but all cash flows net of expenses go to the lender until they are sufficient to pay principal and interest on the restructured loan.

This case study presents information on the Stamford and related office markets (Boston, Hartford, New York, and the nation as a whole). This information will be used to generate plausible scenarios for NOI from the Somerset Associates building over the decade from 1990 to 2000. These scenarios will determine whether the lender would be better off taking the building in foreclosure or allowing the current owners to retain active interest in managing the building.

Stamford Office Market

The Stamford office market is defined by Coldwell Banker to include Norwalk and Bridgeport; that is, the Fairfield County office market is considered as a single entity. The Stamford market (hereafter, synonymous with Fairfield County) is considered to be a suburban area within the greater New York office market. The 1990 vacancy rate in Stamford of 28.9 percent (according to Coldwell Banker's Commercial Office Vacancy Index) was similar to the suburban vacancy rates in Hartford and New York. It was higher than suburban vacancy rates nationwide (about 22 percent in June 1990) and in Boston (12 percent in June 1990). The Building Owners and Managers Association data indicated that effective rents and operating expenses in Stamford were similar to those reported by the SA building.[6] Therefore, I concluded that the SA building was experiencing typical rents, expenses, vacancy rates, and NOI for a building of its size and age.

Since market rental rates have been declining, market rents are below the effective rents collected. Like other buildings in Stamford, the SA building has several leases that were negotiated in the 1986–89 period, when market rents were much higher than now. In 1991, vacant space could be expected to rent in the $15–$18 per year range ($1.25 to $1.50 per month), as opposed to $29 per year ($2.42

per month) on space rented previously. In addition, absorption rates were low, so any rental could be expected to take a long time.

The scenarios here assume a high statistical correlation between the Stamford office market and the national office market. That is, I believed that movements in absorption, rents, and vacancy rates experienced in Stamford would approximate those experienced nationwide. This assumption was supported by a high statistical correlation (simple correlation coefficient equal to .85) between the national office market absorption and the New York office market absorption (Coldwell Banker, "Market Watch," June 1990). Similarly, another regional office market, Boston, had a correlation coefficient of .7 with the nation.

National Office Market

At the time of this case study (1991), the most recent available forecast for the national office market was from Coldwell Banker's "Market Watch," June 1990. Coldwell Banker expected vacancy rates to remain high, as they had over the three to four years previous. But real (inflation adjusted) returns to investments in the office market had been increasing from their very low levels of a few years previous. Coldwell Banker predicted further increases over the next 3–5 years. Given that, in 1990, real returns were 3–4 percent of invested capital, they were expected to increase to 7 percent or 8 percent. That is, real returns were expected to double over the next several years as inflation caused rents to increase at a faster rate than costs.[7]

In 1988, Wheaton and Torto forecast the national office market to 1993. In 1990, the recession that they predicted had reached the northeastern United States. The decline in real rents had become a reality as rents grew more slowly than the general level of inflation.

In 1986, Birch forecast the Stamford and national office markets. Like Wheaton and Torto (1988), he saw a slowdown in absorption as the shift to office occupations declined. Thus, Birch suggested that real rents would decline and vacancies would remain high. The determination of a normal level of vacancies in this market is discussed in the upcoming subsection on "Vacancy Rates."

Methods

The local and national market information discussed here, combined with information from the SA building, produced optimistic and pessimistic scenarios on cash flows and then-current values from the SA property. There are four components to these scenarios:

1. Vacancy rate forecasts;
2. Trends in potential gross income (PGI);
3. Trends in total operating expenses, including property insurance and property taxes; and
4. Investor information and loan terms, including negative amortization.

Vacancy Rates

Reasonable expectations about vacancy rates are tied to normal or "structural" vacancy rates in the marketplace. The normal vacancy rate is optimal from the point of view of management and tenants. That is, the market is in equilibrium at the normal vacancy rate and there is no tendency for it to increase or decline.

Economists are unanimous in the opinion that the normal vacancy rate increased over 1980–1990 because of lower interest rates and the structural shift toward office employment and toward the suburbs; none believe that single-digit vacancy rates are likely in the foreseeable future. A study by Voith and Crone (1988) provided extensive empirical estimates on vacancy rates in downtown and suburban markets, including the Boston and New York markets. Voith and Crone showed the normal or structural vacancy rates trending upward in the New York suburbs. Their data indicated that the normal vacancy rate in the New York suburbs was between 15 percent and 25 percent, with a most likely scenario being about 20 percent. Furthermore, they showed that the New York and Boston markets adjust fairly rapidly to the normal vacancy rate. Thus, when the market is adjusting toward equilibrium, it should approach the normal vacancy rate within a one-and-a-half-year period.

Potential Gross Income

Potential gross income is tied to the rate of inflation. The studies discussed previously suggested that PGI will decline by about 1 percent per year *in real terms* through the late 1990s. A robust economy with high demand for office space would cause PGI to grow at the rate of inflation. Thus, my optimistic scenario is for constant real rents over the foreseeable future.

My forecast for inflation is simply a long-run average rate of inflation in the United States. Over the past 26 years (1964–1990), the average annual rate of inflation has been 5.3 percent. This is above the current inflation rate, especially in view of the recession that began in 1990. Thus, it appears reasonable to project rents to grow 3 percent for 2 years, 4 percent for 1 year, and 5.3 percent over the following 7 years.

Operating Expenses and Investor Information

I used BOMA data to project operating expenses. The strategy here was the same as for inflation: BOMA data yielded a 26-year average increase in operating expenses of 4.5 percent per year. Again, this was close to recent trends in the Stamford market. Therefore, I projected this rate of increase over the next 10 years.

The lender, First Bank, was seeking to acquire the SA building, whereas the borrower was seeking to restructure the loan so as to allow continued ownership interest by SA associates. The original loan agreement allowed the borrower to convert to a fixed-rate loan at 3 percent over the one-year Treasury bill rate. At the time of Chapter 11 proceedings (1990), this interest rate would have been 9.5 percent. Therefore, 9.5 percent was used as the interest rate on the loan and as the discount rate for finding present value of future cash flows.[8]

The tax bracket for this analysis was set at zero. Both the lender and the borrower had financial losses, so they had no tax liability. Although future liability was a possibility, the lender could offset this by carrying forward the current tax losses. Finally, the cost of the project to the lender was the amount of the loan, $4,000,000.

Cram-Down Analysis

Figure 7.4 summarizes the market assumptions supported by the preceding analysis. A three-year lease term was used because it was desirable to keep the lease term short, given the relatively low level of market rents. (Note that existing space was earning $26 per square foot, whereas new space could be leased at an effective rent of $16.50.)

Figure 7.5 summarizes the results of the most-likely scenario. Under this scenario, the loan balance would build up to about $4,700,000 in January of year 4 of operation. This is because the current cash flow from the building, about $18,000 per month, would be insufficient to pay interest on the loan, about $32,000 per month.

Figure 7.4 SCENARIO FOR SOMERSET ASSOCIATES CRAM-DOWN ANALYSIS

Lease term (years)		3
Average annual rent per square foot ($)		16.50
Quarters to stabilized occupancy		12
Stabilized occupancy (%)		85
Net rentable area in square feet		24,887
Percentage preleased		70.5
Leasing commission (%)		6.0
Tenant improvement cost per square foot ($)		20
Expenses per square foot occupied ($)		9
Expenses per square foot vacant ($)		8
Income growth rate (%)	5.3%	0.03[a]
Expense growth rate (%)	4.0%	0.04[b]
Discount rate (required return) (%)		9.5
Resale cap rate (%)		10.5
Mortgage interest rate (%)		9.5
Cost per square foot ($)		125
Cost of land ($)		900,000
Cost of completed project: land plus construction ($)		4,010,875
Loan amount ($)		4,000,000
Loan term (years)		25
Commercial or residential (C or R)		C
Tax bracket (local, state, and federal) (%)		0
Required loan payment ($)		34,947.87
Yearly depreciation ($)		98,757.94

Notes: Most-likely assumptions are supported by market analysis.
a. Growth for income and expenses, first two years: .03 = 3 percent; 5.3% thereafter.
b. Growth for income and expenses, third year: .04 = 4 percent; 4% thereafter.

But, after January of year 4, the projected loan balance would gradually decline, to about $4,200,000 at the end of year 10. At this time, the building is projected to sell for about $22,500,000, so the loan could be repaid with interest at 9.5 percent. Under these most-likely assumptions, the present value of all future net cash flows is about $9,000,000. Since interest and principal payments have been subtracted for net cash flows, the borrower has equity of $9,000,000. Thus, these assumptions suggest that it would be worthwhile to continue holding onto the building in expectation of improving market conditions.

These assumptions should be compared to current (1990) market conditions. In the current market, there are very few buyers for office buildings of any type. Since the SA property is in financial difficulty, it will be very difficult to find a buyer. Appraisers hired by First Bank valued the property in today's market at between $2 million

Figure 7.5 MOST-LIKELY CRAM-DOWN ANALYSIS RESULTS

	Year 1	Year 2	Year 3	Year 4	Year 5	Year 6	Year 7	Year 8	Year 9	Year 10
Effective gross income ($)	467,980	488,431	509,549	973,733	1,014,479	1,057,439	1,763,225	1,810,977	1,861,323	2,688,453
Expenses ($)	220,309	228,266	237,793	248,097	258,205	268,725	279,673	291,068	302,926	315,268
Net operating income (1 − 2) ($)	247,671	260,165	271,756	725,635	756,274	788,714	1,483,552	1,519,910	1,558,397	2,373,185
Initial leasing commission ($)	3,622	3,732	3,866	30,837	2,134	2,250	36,138	2,501	2,637	42,352
Tenant improvement cost ($)	22,053	24,057	24,057	187,482	12,029	12,029	187,482	12,029	12,029	187,482
Cash flow before debt service (3 − 4 − 5) ($)	221,997	232,375	243,833	507,316	742,111	774,435	1,259,931	1,505,380	1,543,731	2,143,351
Interest expense on loan ($)	387,072	403,087	419,501	442,017	436,845	429,531	432,776	424,716	414,717	409,222
Payment (principal plus interest) to amortize loan ($)	429,528	452,255	476,440	508,847	510,541	510,541	524,223	525,466	525,466	532,629
Additional financing required ($)	165,076	170,711	175,668	181,807	0	0	123,566	0	0	54,154
Loan balance ($)	4,165,076	4,335,787	4,511,455	4,631,567	4,557,871	4,476,861	4,516,084	4,415,334	4,304,584	4,245,042

Notes: Table gives annual summaries of monthly estimates. Additional financing required in years 7 and 10 comes from the first month of the year when leasing expenses, tenant improvements, and interest expenses are much larger than NOI. Additional financing represents the need for a source of capital that is paid at a market rate of return.

and $3 million. Thus, sale in today's market would create a loss of between $1 million and $2 million for First Bank.

In summary, it does not appear worthwhile to sell the property in today's depressed market. Reasonable assumptions suggest that the market will improve, allowing the lender to recover the full amount of the loan with interest. This is supported by the lack of new office construction and the presence of some positive absorption which is likely to cause real rental rates to increase by 1997.

A question arises about the motivation of the borrower if the loan is restructured to allow negative amortization (i.e., the loan balance is allowed to build up during the first three years when cash flows are insufficient to pay interest). Under the most-likely assumptions, the borrower is motivated by the extra value that remains in the building at the end of year 10. In present-value terms, the borrower has an equity interest equal to the $9,000,000 present value of future net cash flows. Note that net cash flows become substantially positive in year 5 (figure 7.5), so equity investors will see cash returns at that time. Furthermore, the borrower will earn a normal rate of return for managing the property. Finally, the borrower has an option on more favorable outcomes for the property. For example, it is possible that absorption will be greater than anticipated and that inflation will cause rent and net operating income to rise faster than expected. In this case, the borrower will have substantial value in the building, whereas the borrower has no value if the lender forecloses on the property.

Pessimistic Scenarios

During court proceedings, First Bank argued that the assumptions made under the most-likely scenario were too optimistic. They argued that the building would have difficulty competing against newer structures, so that the rate of increase in rental income would be much slower than indicated by the most-likely scenario. Therefore, some pessimistic scenarios were constructed.

Figure 7.6 indicates the assumptions made under a pessimistic scenario. This scenario assumed a 3 percent rate of growth in rental income and in expenses for three years and then a 4 percent rate per year after that. Thus, rental income was never projected to grow faster than expenses, and the projected rates of growth were very low relative to historical inflation rates.

Under this scenario, the loan balance would grow to about $4,700,000 at the beginning of year 4; thereafter, it would gradually

Figure 7.6 PESSIMISTIC SCENARIO: SOMERSET ASSOCIATES CRAM-DOWN
ANALYSIS

Lease term (years)	3
Average annual rent per square foot ($)	16.50
Quarters to stabilized occupancy	12
Stabilized occupancy (%)	85
Net rentable area in square feet	24,887
Percentage preleased	70.5
Leasing commission (%)	6.0
Tenant improvement cost per square foot ($)	20
Expenses per square foot occupied ($)	9
Expenses per square foot vacant ($)	8
Income growth rate (%)	3% 0.03[a]
Expense growth rate (%)	3% 0.03[b]
Discount rate (required return %)	9.5
Resale cap rate (%)	10.5
Mortgage interest rate (%)	9.5
Cost per square foot ($)	125
Cost of land ($)	900,000
Cost of completed project: land plus construction ($)	4,010,875
Loan amount ($)	4,000,000
Loan term (years)	25
Commercial or residential (C or R)	C
Tax bracket (local, state, and federal) (%)	0
Required loan payment ($)	34,947.87
Yearly depreciation ($)	98,757.94

Notes:4a. Growth for income and expenses, first two years is .03 (3%) per year.
b. Growth for income and expenses, third year is .03 (3%).

reduce to about $4,300,000 at the end of year 10. The present value
of all future cash flows is about $5,000,000, so the lender is repaid
with interest at 9.5 percent and the borrower has substantial equity
remaining in the project. Thus, restructuring would make sense under
these pessimistic assumptions.

Finally, a very pessimistic scenario was constructed. Under this
scenario, there would be zero growth in costs and rent for 3 years.
Thereafter, the growth is only 3 percent per year. Under this scenario,
the loan balance builds up to $5,400,000 and is reduced to $5,000,000
at the end of year 10. The borrower still has an equity interest of
$1,200,000 (present value of future net cash flows). Since there
appears to be little risk that the actual outcome will be worse than
this very pessimistic scenario, it appears that the lender can be repaid
with interest while the borrower still retains substantial equity. Thus,
everyone is better off underrestructuring, whereas both the lender

and borrower will lose substantial amounts of money under foreclosure and immediate sale of the property.[9]

SUMMARY AND CONCLUSIONS

This chapter introduces the additional information needed to tie the knot between office market research and investment, development, appraisal, lending, and public policy decisions. This additional information includes loan terms, investor characteristics (e.g., tax bracket and required return on equity) and building characteristics (e.g., land and construction costs).

A spreadsheet was used to demonstrate the implications of market analysis for net operating income, cash flows, loan requirements, ability to repay the loan, income taxes, and the present value of future cash flows. Although the spreadsheet used is moderately complex, it has the advantage of allowing the user to see how the calculations are made. Therefore, it allows easy modification of the basic assumptions of the analysis. These advantages can be compared to commercial investment analysis software, which operate on the black box principle.

The spreadsheet was used to evaluate the feasibility of new office construction. The implications of optimistic, pessimistic, and most-likely assumptions based on market analysis can be derived for a proposed new office building (see figure 7.2). This provides a simple framework for evaluating the risks associated with investment, lending, and appraisal decisions.

The model was used for lease analysis. In the depressed market conditions assumed for this example, shorter leases provide better results for landlords than longer leases. When two-year leases are compared to five-year leases, the former require considerably less capital (i.e., the maximum loan balance is smaller) and produce considerably higher equity for the investors. This occurs because the shorter leases allow landlords to take advantage of rising rents. This advantage more than compensates for higher vacancy rates, higher leasing expenses, and higher tenant improvement costs. "Workout" situations are common in office markets. In this situation, a lender must decide whether to hold and operate a property or whether to sell it on the market. Information about absorption of vacant space, rental rates, costs and growth in rental rates, and total expenses is essential in these decisions.

A case study of a workout situation is analyzed with the spread-sheet software. In this case, the borrower is in Chapter 11 bankruptcy proceedings, seeking a restructuring of the loan (cram-down analysis). If the lender were to take the property today and sell it on the open market, the lender would realize a loss of between $1,000,000 and $2,000,000, and the borrower would lose all of the investment in the property. The reason for this is that the current market is very depressed, with few buyers and few lenders.

Pessimistic market assumptions were used with the spreadsheet to show that workout would provide a better alternative for this property. Even with pessimistic assumptions, the borrower would be motivated to retain an interest in the property (i.e., to manage it efficiently), and the lender would be repaid with interest at 9.5 percent.

We were unable to find any reasonable market assumptions that produce different results. Thus, the case study provides an example of effective use of market analysis for office buildings.

Notes

1. The model, RENTTAX.WK1, was programmed in LOTUS Macro language by Richard Wassmundt, while he was an MBA student, and me.

2. Stabilized occupancy is the normal and reasonable occupancy rate that can be expected for a building of a given type in the area.

3. Fifteen percent is a reasonable estimate of the natural vacancy rate for many cities in the early 1990s.

4. These growth rates are assumed to be constant over 10 years in this simple example; of course, they could be made to change over time.

5. Industry sources indicate that these terms were typical at the time this was written in 1991.

6. Effective rents are those actually earned as opposed to those stated in the rental contract. Collection losses, free rent, and related concessions reduce effective rent.

7. At the time of this case study (1991), inflation was expected to increase as part of the typical cyclical recovery from recession.

8. Since the lender entered into an agreement allowing for a 9.5 percent interest rate, it is reasonable to assume that this was the most the lender could expect to earn on this loan. Therefore, no risk adjustment was allowed in the discount rate.

9. The lender argued that Wall Street, and banking regulators, required sale of the property at a loss. The preceding analysis suggests that this would not be rational behavior.

COMMENTATOR'S REMARKS

It is the policy of the AREUEA Monograph Committee to select outside commentators to provide comments to be used by the author in making revisions to the manuscript. In addition, commentators are asked to provide brief remarks on aspects of the literature that may not be fully covered in the main text. The commentators are selected based on their area of expertise and on their published research.

For this monograph, two sets of commentators' remarks have been solicited. The first set of remarks, by Michael Raper and Keith Ihlanfeldt, reports on recent developments in research designed to illuminate the spatial microfoundations of office space demand. Raper and Ihlanfeldt suggest that the next steps in understanding office location will require disaggregation of office functions into rather detailed categories based on theoretical differences in the motivation for choice. Such disaggregation includes questions of firm size, organizational structure and skill mix of labor, as well as industrial characteristics.

The second set of remarks, by Kenneth Rosen, illustrates the way in which a veteran office market researcher produces aggregate forecasts of office space demand. This macro view of the office market complements the discussion of local office demand projection provided by Clapp in the main text.

TOWARD UNDERSTANDING HOW OFFICE-LOCATION DECISIONS DIFFER

Michael Raper and Keith R. Ihlanfeldt

According to chapter 4, "economic theory provides a framework for explaining broad patterns of office location and changes over time in those locations. However, . . . it has turned a blind eye to much institutional detail that is important for office location." Economic theories of office location have indeed thus far failed to fully utilize the substantial contributions of geographers, planners, and others who have written on the subject; one hopes this is the result of a slow hand rather than a blind eye. Considering the current interest in understanding issues such as "why a given type of office employment is particularly suited to a given location" (chapter 4, this volume), additional effort needs to be directed toward further development and testing of economic theories of office location.

At present, there is no formal economic theory of office location housed in a general equilibrium model of urban land use. Nevertheless, we believe much progress can be made toward understanding office markets by modifying existing models of office location. Clapp (1980), Long and colleagues (1984), and Ihlanfeldt and Raper (1990) have tested economic models of intraurban office location. Although the empirical approaches of these authors differ, their underlying theoretical models have much in common. As mentioned earlier in this monograph, these studies indicate that the major factors influencing office location are agglomeration economies, labor and other factor costs, the cost of maintaining contact with customers and suppliers, political factors, and amenities.

Taken together, the results from these studies are most useful in helping developers and planners understand where office development is likely to occur. However, they offer little insight to the building owner or leasing agent with regard to what types of office use would be most attracted to a particular site. The primary reason for this shortcoming is the level of abstraction in most economic models of office location. To date, researchers have tended to concentrate on the similarities rather than the differences in office users in attempting to understand their location behavior. Although all office users may be similar in that they are "desk-loving animals," most are indeed very different animals whose location behavior reflects those differences.

A much better understanding of office-location choices and the dynamics of office markets could be obtained by investigating how office-location behavior varies for different types of office users. To that end, this essay draws upon economic theory to consider how intraurban office-location decisions are likely to differ among office users. We also report the results of some of our work in this area. We hope this leads to additional research that increases understanding of office markets and provides a better answer to what types of office use will be attracted to a particular location.

DIFFERENCES BETWEEN OFFICE USERS THAT AFFECT LOCATION CHOICE

The production of office services is similar for all types of office users, in that the same inputs are required (i.e., office space, office equipment, labor, and information from suppliers and customers). If it is assumed that individual office users are price takers in input markets, then the spatial variation of input prices causes office users to value particular locations differently. Indeed, for both profit-maximizing and nonprofit organizations, each of the major factors influencing office location mentioned earlier can be analyzed in terms of its effect through input prices.

If office users faced no competition for urban land from other users and all office users were identical, then locational advantages would be capitalized into land prices, leaving individual office users indifferent among locations. However, offices must compete with residential, retail, and other users for urban land. Office users capture land for office use only when their bids exceed those of other users and office use is not prohibited by zoning. In the same way that residential, retail, and office users have different valuations or bid-rents for particular locations, different types of office users also have different valuations for particular locations.

Among the factors causing different types of office users to have different valuations for individual locations are type of industry, organizational structure, size, age, and optimizing behavior. We turn first to the question of how office-location decisions differ by industry.

Industry

Office-location decisions can be expected to vary considerably by industry because of differences in the importance of access to labor and other inputs, agglomeration economies, and access to customers. To address how individual office-location decisions differ by industry, it is useful to distinguish between "office" and "nonoffice" industries. An industry where the primary production facility is a detached office building may be referred to as an office industry and individual producers as office firms. Of the concentrations of office employment mentioned in chapter 1, this definition includes finance, insurance, and real estate; professional, legal, and most business services; health services; educational and social services; membership organizations; and government. Nonoffice industries include those such as manufacturing where the primary production facility is not a detached office building. Firms in nonoffice industries are also office users in that their sales and central administrative functions are performed in offices separate from production facilities.

ACCESS TO LABOR AND OTHER INPUTS

It is primarily differences in the production functions of firms in individual office industries that cause those firms to have different sensitivities to spatial variation in input prices and, as a result, different valuations for particular office locations. Production functions vary among office industries because of differences in technology and specific input requirements unique to individual industries.

The nonuniform distribution of labor and other inputs across an urban area causes the cost of using these inputs to vary at different office locations. Wage rates vary spatially due to differences in commuting costs and nonwage attributes of the work location. As a result, office locations with good access to a certain type of labor important in the production of a particular office service will be attractive to firms producing that service. For example, engineering services should be more attracted to locations with good access to the homes of professional labor than credit reporting and collection services, because the former is produced with a much higher proportion of professional labor.

Long (1984) and Ihlanfeldt and Raper (1990) found that proximity to managerial and professional labor is an important determinant of office-location choice. Neither of these studies looked at differences among industries in the importance of proximity to labor. However, using the same empirical approach as Ihlanfeldt and Raper, Raper (1988) found that proximity to managerial and professional labor is a significant (at the .05 level) determinant of office-location choice for new firms in miscellaneous services but not for new firms in business services. Miscellaneous services include engineering and architectural services, as well as accounting and auditing services— industries employing a high proportion of managerial and professional labor. On the other hand, business services include credit reporting and collection and stenographic services—industries employing a lower proportion of managerial and professional labor.

Access to inputs other than labor may also be important in determining office-location choice in some industries. Real estate is an office industry with a need for access to a unique input. Property for sale or lease may be considered a necessary input in the production of real estate services. Potential customers must be shown properties before agents can negotiate an agreement between buyer and seller. Likewise, appraisers must view properties before providing appraisals for banks or individuals. Consequently, convenient access to available properties should be an important determinant of location for real estate offices. Raper (1988) found that new real estate firms are attracted to office locations with access to expressways.

AGGLOMERATION ECONOMIES

There is tendency in some office industries for firms to cluster together with other firms in that industry. This is particularly true for health services and legal services, where the motivation may be the need for convenient access to shared inputs such as hospitals and courthouses. In the case of legal services, it may also reflect the need for frequent face-to-face meetings that are held outside the courthouse between attorneys from different firms. Raper (1988) found that new firms in health services and legal services chose office locations with high concentrations of employment in those industries.

The clustering of different types of health services reflects the fact that some health services are used as inputs in the production of others. For example, physicians and dentists require access to the services of medical and dental laboratories and may need to refer some patients to specialists for part of their treatment. In addition, the clustering of health services in medical office buildings and office parks is in part due to a common need for office space that has been modified to accommodate the unique requirements of health services.

Firms in health services and other office industries may also benefit from locating near similar firms in much the same way that retailers in small towns benefit from proximity to each other. Namely, by establishing working relationships with other firms in the same industry, office firms can specialize and refer customers to each other. In this way, they help customers minimize the search costs of shopping for a particular service and thereby increase their attractiveness to customers. This behavior may be important to the owners of small firms that wish to maintain their autonomy by remaining small.

Finally, clustering of office firms in the same industry may also occur when prestige locations are important in attracting certain clients. A prestige address may be a requirement for law, advertising, and brokerage firms that wish to attract customers looking for companies with a proven success record. Prestige locations convey an image of success by informing potential customers that tenants are accomplished enough in their fields to afford the higher rents of a prestige address.

ACCESS TO CUSTOMERS

Access to customers can be an important factor in differentiating office-location choice among industries, for two reasons. First, for many office services that are sold locally, better access to customers means higher demand. This is especially true for such services as real estate, insurance, tax preparation, travel arrangement, and investment services, where customer contact is often initiated by walk-in-traffic. Thus, such office services are likely to locate in shopping centers or low-density office developments rather than in high-rise buildings where walk-in traffic is discouraged.

A second reason why access to customers as a determinant of office-location choice can differ among industries is that some office services are unique to individual buyers and require face-to-face meetings with customers to obtain information that only the customer can provide. Such face-to-face meetings can be considered a necessary input in the production of those office services. Moreover, the cost of transporting employees to face-to-face meetings with customers is lower at locations that provide better access to customers. Because the significance of face-to-face meetings with customers varies across industries, the importance of access will likewise vary.

In general, the more specialized the services to individual customers, the more information is required from customers in face-to-face meetings and the more important is customer access in determining office location. Business services such as consulting, advertising, and computer services; and miscellaneous services such as engineering and accounting services are typically unique to individual customers and therefore can be expected to require frequent face-to-face meetings with customers. Raper (1988) found that new office firms in business services and miscellaneous services are attracted to areas of employment growth.

As noted by Marshall (1983), business services are often exported. For those firms with customers outside the metropolitan area, office locations with access to expressways or the airport will provide better access to distant customers. Raper (1988) found that access to expressways and to the airport has a marginally significant (at the .10 level) influence on the office-location choices of new firms in business services.

Office services sold to individuals differ from business services in two ways likely to influence office-location choice. First, most office services sold to individuals are produced for local markets and are therefore less likely to seek locations that facilitate travel outside the metropolitan area. Second, many office services sold to individuals differ only slightly from customer to customer. The more standardized the service, the less important are face-to-face contacts with established customers likely to be. In many cases, adequate information from such customers may be obtained over the telephone, through the mail, or by fax. Communications between established customers and insurance agents, travel agents, and stockbrokers are often handled routinely without the need for face-to-face meetings. Nevertheless, office firms in these industries may need occasional contact with their established customers to maintain good relationships. Meetings of this type are often held after work or during lunch for the convenience of clients. Raper (1988) found access to expressways and proximity to eating and drinking establishments to be significant determinants of location choice for new firms in insurance and transportation services (passenger travel arrangement).

Organizational Structure

Office-location decisions can also be expected to vary by organizational structure. For example, Ihlanfeldt and Raper (1990) found that newly established "independent" office firms and new branches of established firms displayed distinctly different location behaviors. In particular, we found that new independent offices are attracted to locations convenient to support services, whereas new branches are not. This offers support for Marshall's (1983) contention that new independent office firms must rely on outside suppliers for some inputs that branch offices can obtain through their organizations.

Another difference we found between the two types of firms is that access to customers is more important to new branch offices. This result is not surprising, since better access to new customers is likely the motivation behind opening a new branch. Since new branches are less concerned with the need to choose locations with access to suppliers of some inputs, branches should have more flexibility than independent firms in choosing locations close to customers.

Finally, we found that new branch offices are more attracted than new independent offices to locations that offer amenities for employees and access to rail transit stations. Our explanation for these results is that such locations might reduce labor turnover if some employees were transferred when the new branch was opened. Locations with positive nonwage attributes such as amenities for employees (shopping, restaurants, entertainment, and so forth) and lower commuting costs should be more appealing to employees required to transfer to the new branch.

Besides the differences that we found between new branches and new independent office firms in their choices of location, three additional observations can be made that relate to organizational structure. First, the office-location choices of corporate and regional headquarters containing central administrative functions are likely to be strongly influenced by access to labor and factors related to communicating with other parts of the organization. Access to the airport and availability of hotels for out-of-town employees and clients are considerations that should affect the office-location choices of those headquarters with a strong need to maintain face-to-face contact with employees and clients in other cities. Headquarter offices may also be attracted to "smart" buildings with capabilities for extensive networking of computers and facilities that make it convenient for companies to substitute teleconferences for meetings requiring intercity travel.

Second, in addition to having their central administrative functions housed in offices, nonoffice industries also have regional sales offices. These offices should be very footloose in choosing their locations within an urban area. Given their limited need for support services, as well as the number of locations with similar accessibility to customers and production facilities located outside the urban area, the office-location decisions of regional sales offices are likely to be strongly influenced by proximity to the residences of sales personnel.

Finally, access to labor and the availability of low-cost space may be dominant factors in determining office-location choices for such activities as the labor-intensive billing and collection functions of banks, insurance carriers, and utilities. These activities may also require office space that has been specially designed or modified to accommodate the unique data processing and communications needs of these office users.

Size

According to Scott (1983), the labor-intensive production of many nonstandardized office services limits the efficient size of these firms relative to firms in capital-intensive industries such as manufacturing where there are significant economies of scale. Moreover, it is easy to find firms of widely divergent size in individual office industries, which suggests constant returns to scale over a considerable range of output. However, while the relative efficiency of different size office firms in a particular industry may be similar, their location behavior is likely to differ for several reasons.

First, small firms should be more dependent on outside suppliers for some inputs in the same way that independent offices are more dependent on outside suppliers than branch offices. For example, small firms should be less likely than large firms to produce services such as accounting and bookkeeping internally and therefore should have stronger preferences for locations with good access to those services. Raper (1988) found that proximity to support services has a significant influence on the location choices of new office firms with less than 6 employees, but not on the location choices of new office firms with more than 10 employees.

Second, labor may be more specialized in larger office firms. Thus, large offices might need to draw from a wider geographic area to fill their labor needs. As a result, larger offices should be more likely to choose more central locations than small offices or to choose locations with access to expressways or rail transit. Raper (1988) found that access to expressways has a significant affect on the location choices of large offices but not on the location choices of small offices. In addition, access to rail transit stations was found to have a marginally significant effect on location choice for large offices but not for small offices.

Another possible difference in the location behavior of large and small offices is that larger offices might be less likely to relocate as often as small offices. Over time, changes in the factors that influence location choice cause the locations of established office firms to become less optimal. However, relocation will not occur until the additional profit resulting from a move exceeds the costs of moving. There are at least four reasons why small firms will relocate more frequently. First, large office firms may be less likely to relocate owing to higher moving costs. For example, if larger firms do indeed need to draw from a larger geographic area to fill more specialized labor needs, then relocation could prove more costly to them in terms of higher labor turnover as some employees are faced with longer commuting trips than they are willing to make.

Second, small offices may relocate more often than large offices because they serve smaller markets. Having relatively few customers relocate, go out of business, or carry their trade elsewhere can result in a shift of an office firms's market center. Relocations triggered by such a shift may be less likely for larger firms with customers dispersed over larger market areas.

Third, lack of adequate office space may cause small firms to relocate more often than large firms. There is considerable evidence that most employment growth comes from expansion of small firms. If smaller office firms are more likely to expand than large office firms, then small firms should be more likely to relocate if adequate space is not available at existing locations.

Finally, lack of available space at more attractive locations could significantly hinder large office firms that wish to relocate but may have little effect on small office firms. For example, the space requirements of large corporate headquarters may impose severe limitations on their location choices, particularly in sluggish office markets where large amounts of new space are added infrequently. However, size can have its advantages in expanding office markets. Large office users may be in a unique position to negotiate favorable leases as space becomes available in new buildings, because they often bring other tenants with them and because leasing to large tenants reduces the search costs of finding suitable tenants to fill a new building.

Age and Length of Tenure

An office firm's location behavior should also be related to where the firm is in its life cycle. In particular, the location decisions of new firms should differ significantly from those of established firms. Face-to-face meetings with suppliers of inputs should be especially important to new office firms who may be dealing with individual suppliers for the first time. Thus, new independent offices are likely to choose locations with good access to those services that cannot be provided internally. New offices of this type may also choose locations where similar firms are located, in an effort to reduce the search costs of finding a suitable location by observing the behavior of similar firms.

According to Scott (1983), new firms benefit from locating near firms in their own industry for two other reasons. First, locating near similar firms may provide new firms with better information on market prices. Second, it facilitates subcontracting with other firms when demand is unexpectedly high or when it is simply more efficient to subcontract part of a job to another firm. Locations that facilitate subcontracting should be particularly appealing to new firms because of the uncertainty they face with regard to demand and their unfamiliarity with scheduling production.

Given the limited information with which new office firms choose their initial locations, many will want to relocate as they acquire the additional knowledge that permits a better-informed location choice. Relocating firms should give less weight to some factors that were influential in making their initial location choices. For example, as maturing firms become more knowledgeable about market prices, their need to locate near other firms in the same industry should diminish. Mature firms should also engage in less subcontracting and require fewer face-to-face meetings with subcontractors as the process becomes more routine.

Once a better-informed location choice is made, subsequent relocations should become less likely over time. In fact, a certain inertia may develop that increases with length of tenure at a particular site. Efficiency may increase as employees become familiar with doing business at a particular location. Moreover, some employees may change their residential locations to make them more convenient to work, once they perceive the office location to be permanent. Consequently, relocating to a new site a substantial distance away could prove more costly the longer the firm remains at a particular site. For these reasons, the locational stability of office firms should increase with their age and length of tenure, other things being equal.

Optimizing Behavior

Most of the office users in the industries listed previously can be assumed to be motivated by a desire to maximize profits, and therefore can be expected to choose their locations accordingly. However, the same cannot be said for the location choices of membership organizations, social services, and government.

Historically, there has been a strong tendency for government offices and many nonprofit organizations to choose central-city office locations. For social services and government offices that serve the needs of the poor, central-city locations may offer the best access to users of those services, owing to the availability of public transportation. Also, because of budget constraints, many government offices and nonprofit organizations often locate in less-expensive office space available in older, central-city office markets.

Government offices that export their services may choose central-city office locations for other reasons. First, they may have strong linkages to other government offices, particularly in the case of state and local government. Thus, the clustering of government offices reduces the cost of face-to-face contacts between employees of different branches of government. Second, governments and nonprofit organizations often have strong affirmative action commitments that are best served at central-city locations convenient to public transportation. Finally, the choice of central-city office locations may reflect a conscious effort by government to promote economic development in central cities to help maintain their economic viability.

There is also a strong tendency for municipal government offices in the suburbs to cluster together. This location behavior could likewise be the result of strong linkages between branches of local government or could reflect attempts to minimize the transportation and time costs of consumers of local government services. For those services offered at only one location within a jurisdiction, a common location reduces the cost of obtaining more than one service at a time and reduces the search costs of residents who are obtaining services for the first time.

SUMMARY AND CONCLUSION

In summary, there are many reasons why the location decisions of different types of office users can be expected to differ. Understanding how office-location decisions differ is essential to understanding what types of office use will be attracted to particular locations and how office markets change over time. These issues have practical relevance to building owners and leasing agents searching for suitable tenants and public officials who must anticipate the evolution of particular office markets.

The primary purpose of this essay has been to draw attention to a neglected area of research. We have presented examples of how a number of factors cause differences in the location behaviors of various types of office users. Much additional empirical work remains, however, to determine how important these and other institutional factors are in explaining how office-location decisions differ.

DEMAND FOR OFFICE SPACE: A FORECAST FOR THE 1990s

Kenneth T. Rosen

This essay describes a four-part approach to forecasting demand for office space. First, I analyze the employment sectors that constitute office employment. Second, I forecast the employment in these sectors to derive a forecast of office employment. Third, I analyze the space intensity of employment. Fourth, I multiply the employment forecast by the space intensity coefficient to generate a demand forecast. To place bounds on the forecast for office space, I examine a range of both the employment forecasts and the space intensity forecasts. This method provides a base forecast together with sensitivity bounds around that forecast.

DEMAND FOR OFFICE SPACE

Demand for office space is driven by office employment, which consists of employment in the following sectors:

☐ Finance, insurance, and real estate
☐ Business services
☐ Medical doctors, dentists, and other health practitioners
☐ Legal services
☐ Membership organizations
☐ Engineering and architectural services
☐ Accounting services
☐ Management consulting and public relations services

For a summary of employment growth in these sectors from 1970 to 1990, see table II.1. The table shows that office employment grew at a compound annual rate of 6.4 percent from 1970 to 1980 and a corresponding 3.9 percent from 1980 to 1990.

Table II.1 U.S. OFFICE EMPLOYMENT LEVELS AND GROWTH RATES (IN THOUSANDS, EXCEPT PERCENT)

Sector	1970	1980	1985	1990	1991	2000	Compound Annual Growth Rates (%)		Rosen Forecast 1990–2000	BLS[a] Forecast 1990–2000
							1970–80	1980–90		
Total nonagricultural employment	70,725	91,750	99,546	110,841	108,655	126,123	2.64	1.91	1.30	1.30
Total office employment	5,923	10,989	13,974	16,096	16,238	19,621	6.38	3.89	2.00	—
FIRE[b]	3,712	5,237	6,080	6,813	6,770	7,752	3.50	2.67	1.30	1.30
Finance	1,713	2,549	3,051	3,339	3,302	—	4.05	2.74	—	—
Depository Institutions	1,171	1,858	2,096	2,297	2,267	—	4.73	2.14	—	—
Insurance	1,341	1,697	1,866	2,149	2,130	—	2.38	2.39	—	—
Real estate	659	992	1,163	1,325	1,338	—	4.18	2.94	—	—
Business services	1,676	3,238	4,652	5,035	5,370	6,138	5.81	4.52	2.00	3.40
Membership organizations	—	1,581	1,515	2,417	1,979	2,777	—	4.33	1.40	—
Legal services	236	520	704	939	934	1,179	8.22	6.09	2.30	2.80
Offices and clinics of doctors/dentists	—	1,115	1,424	2,000	1,887	2,795	—	6.02	3.40	3.50
Accounting	—	325	421	526	509	707	—	4.96	3.00	—
Engineering and architecture	299	554	693	782	768	1,051	6.38	3.50	3.00	—
Management and public relations	—	—	—[c]	565	631	710	—	—	2.30	—

Notes: Dashes denote data not available.
a. BLS, Bureau of Labor Statistics.
b. FIRE, finance, insurance, and real estate.
c. Data not available due to Standard Industrial Code change in 1987.

Table II.2 OFFICE EMPLOYMENT GROWTH: UNITED STATES, 1970–2000

	CAGR (%)[a]	Absolute Number per Year (000s)
1970–80	5.27	441.6
1980–85	4.81	597.0
1985–90	2.83	424.4
1990–2000	2.04	359.8

a. CAGR, Compound annual growth rate.

OFFICE EMPLOYMENT GROWTH

For the forecast period, I show the Bureau of Labor Statistics' (BLS) expectations for employment growth, as well as my own. My expectations match those of the BLS fairly well, but my growth anticipations are generally a bit more conservative. The difference is minor except in the business services sector, where the BLS anticipates a compound annual growth rate of 3.4 percent during the forecast period, whereas I anticipate a 2 percent growth rate. I base this growth rate on the relationship of business services growth to total office employment growth. The BLS growth rate for business services exceeds the relationship observed in the 1980s, and for that reason I have reduced the growth expected in this sector.

Table II.2 summarizes office employment growth. The growth rate for office employment in the decade of the 1990s will decline to 2 percent. This decline is the result of many factors. First, the labor force growth throughout the economy will slow as a result of several demographic factors. The growth in female labor force participation is largely behind us in the 1990s. Also, the baby bust generation, with birth years between 1970 and 1980, are the ones entering the labor force in the 1990s. These are the years that birthrates were low, and the resulting growth in the labor force in the 1990s will also be slower than in the 1980s.

Second, the finance, insurance, and real estate sector of employment, which is the largest single user of office space, will undergo further consolidation in the 1990s. Depository institutions will experience consolidation, as a historic wave of mergers, acquisitions, and outright closures of depository institutions occurs during the forecast horizon. The industry structure will be skewed toward fewer, larger, lower-cost providers of services.

The erosion of outdated banking laws, such as the McFadden Act prohibition of interstate services and the Glass-Steagall Act separation of commercial banking from investment banking, means that the financial services industry will change in ways that foster more competition, and thus will further favor the low cost provider. The erosion of these laws, even though their formal demise has been painfully slow in coming, will accelerate the move to a far-different industry structure. The net impact of these changes will be that employment growth in the finance sector will be slower over the course of the 1990s than at any time in the past 20 years.

Employment growth in business services and legal services will slow markedly during the 1990s. The reason, as mentioned earlier, is that business services employment bears a relationship to total office employment, and as total office employment slows, business services employment will also slow. The growth in legal services employment will furthermore decline in the 1990s as a result of price pressure felt from the supply of lawyers, together with increasing resistance on the part of many corporations to the hourly fee-for-service pricing of traditional legal services. There are many people who believe that the country has far too many lawyers.

In other sectors, such as accounting, architecture and engineering, and medical practitioners, employment growth will hold up well during the 1990s, albeit at somewhat slower rates than in the 1980s.

The results of all of these factors are summarized in table II.2. During the 1990s, 359,800 office jobs per year (average) will be added to the labor market. This contrasts with 424,400 during 1985–90, and 597,000 during 1980–85. The absolute number of office jobs added per year in the decade of the 1990s will be even lower than during the decade of the 1970s, when 441,600 office jobs were added per year. Figure II.1 puts these averages into historical perspective.

SPACE INTENSITY OF OFFICE EMPLOYMENT

I now turn to the space intensity of office employment. Estimating space intensity is a major undertaking because of the data problems that accompany such an estimate. The accompanying Appendix presents the technical details underlying the conclusions reached here, the main points of which are as follows.

The space intensity of office employment increased over the past several decades. However, the use of space per office employee stabilized during the late 1980s. Using a crude weighted average across the 67 largest metropolitan areas, I estimate that the space per employee

Figure II.1 ANNUAL OFFICE EMPLOYMENT GROWTH: UNITED STATES,
1973–2000

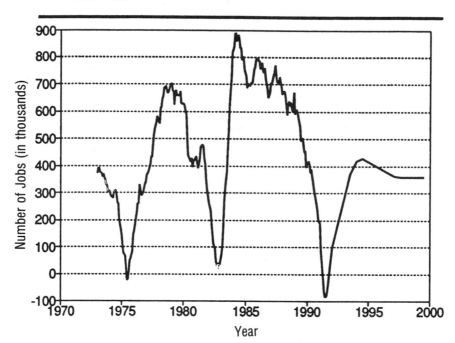

averaged 284 square feet during the 1985–90 period. But in my view
the estimate of 284 square feet per employee is too high because of
the steady decline in growth of office employment during that period.
A statistical analysis of my data showing an unloaded 216 square
feet per employee and a fully loaded 267 square feet per employee
appears to be a reasonable estimate, with an implied load factor of
about 23 percent (see the Appendix).

Several factors argue for a stable to perhaps declining intensity of
space usage per employee during the period forecast. First, at least
during 1993–95, office employment will again be increasing. This
will cause a secular downward bias in the intensity coefficient, much
like the declining office employment gains in the late 1980s resulted
in an upward bias in the coefficient. Second, the new office configuration in many new offices and in older office rehabilitations is modular in nature rather than oriented toward private offices. The modular
configuration permits a much higher density of people per square
foot than does a private office configuration. Third, telecommuting,
or working from home with telephone ties to a corporate office,

will reduce demand for new office space. Although office-consuming employment will grow during the 1990s, the growth of work-at-home arrangements will dampen the demand for office space.

Currently an estimated 5.5 million corporate employees in the United States work at home at least one day a week, and half a million work at home full-time. It is estimated that this sector will grow by 6 percent per year in the 1990s, compared with an overall growth rate of 2 percent per year in office-sector employment. Most telecommuters are workers in information-intensive occupations, such as word processing, data entry, bookkeeping, sales, and marketing. Most telecommuters today also work for small companies of 100 or fewer employees. Workers cite the benefits of telecommuting as follows: reduced stress and time-drain of not commuting; lower transportation, food, and day care expenses; and increased family time. The main impediments to growth of telecommuting have been employers' desire for control and supervision of workers and their jobs, and the need for improved technology to strengthen the tie between home and corporate offices.

Improvements in office technology will increasingly make work at home feasible, with enhanced ability both to send and receive data at home and to participate in meetings via a video telephone connection. Data transmission over telephone lines is growing at a 20 percent annual rate, compared with 6 percent for voice communications. With rising saturation of the U.S. personal computer (PC) market, and increasing sales of modems connecting PCs to telephone lines, telecommuters will constitute an increasing share of office employment. New digital telephone technology will substantially boost the rate of data transmission over telephone lines, leading to economical video-conferencing and stronger electronic connections between home computers and corporate mainframe computers.

As a result of this phenomenon, and cost pressures in the corporate world leading to increasing saturation of modular accommodation of office workers, I do not forecast an increase in the space-intensity of office employment. Rather, I predict a stable rate of 267 square feet per employee. This stability is a dramatic change from the last 50 years, during which the use of office space per employee rose.

FORECAST OF DEMAND IN THE 1990s

Using both the office employment forecast presented here and the space intensity forecast, one can calculate the forecast of net absorp-

Table II.3 FORECAST OF OFFICE SPACE ABSORPTION, 1990–2000

BASE FORECAST
(2 percent employment growth per year)

	1970–80	1980–90	1990–2000
Change in office employment (000s)	5,066	5,107	3,598
Average annual change (000s)	507	511	360
Average space intensity (square feet/employee)	181	239	267
Implied annual absorption (000s square feet)		121,934	
Employment ratio[a]		2	
Annual net absorption (000s square feet)	91,666	188,052	96,057

HIGH EMPLOYMENT GROWTH
(2.75 percent per year)

	1990–2000
Change in office employment (000s)	5,000
Average annual change (000s)	500
Average space intensity (square foot/employee)	267
Annual absorption (000s square feet)	133,489

HIGH EMPLOYMENT GROWTH AND HIGH SPACE INTENSITY

	1990–2000
Change in office employment (000s)	5,000
Average annual change (000s)	500
Average space intensity (square feet/employee)	276
Annual absorption (000s square feet)	137,938

LOW EMPLOYMENT GROWTH AND LOW SPACE INTENSITY
(1.7 percent per year)

	1990–2000
Change in office employment (000s)	2,889
Average annual change (000s)	289
Average space intensity (square feet/employee)	258
Annual absorption (000s square feet)	74,570

a. This ratio results from the fact that employment other than strictly defined office employment uses office space. This ratio yields results consistent with those of Maisel (1989).

tion of office space during the 1990s. Table II.3 shows the forecast for the base case in which office employment grows 2 percent per year for the decade. The annual net absorption of office space in this case is 96.1 million square feet per year.

Several other sensitivities are calculated and presented in table II.3. The "High Employment Growth" case projects office employment to grow at 2.75 percent per year. There are two primary differences in this case: (1) the 1.7 percent per year growth of the finance, insurance, and real estate sector (compared with 1.3 percent per year in the base case) and (2) the 3.5 percent per year growth in business services (compared with a 2 percent per year growth in the base case). In this case, the annual net absorption of office space would be 133.5 million square feet.

The "High Employment Growth and High Space Intensity" case is based on the same office employment assumptions as the "High Employment Growth" case. In addition, the space intensity coefficient is permitted to rise by one standard error during the decade. In this case, the annual net absorption of office space would be 137.9 million square feet.

The final sensitivity examined here combines low office employment growth, 1.7 percent per year, with a space intensity coefficient that is permitted to fall by one standard error during the decade. In this case, the annual net absorption of office space would be 75.6 million square feet.

APPENDIX TO COMMENTARY II

Recent data from the major markets in the United States suggest that in the late 1980s, the space intensity of office employment stabilized. Appendix table II.4 provides estimates from both Rosen (1991) and Maisel (1989) using occupied stock and office employment suggesting that from 1985 to 1990 the space intensity of office employment was nearly constant at an average of 283.7 square feet per employee. During 1984 the space intensity was significantly lower, and during 1991 it was significantly higher. I interpret these data points as differing from the 1985 to 1990 data for cyclical reasons. During 1984, the economy boomed and the gain in office employment reached an all-time high of nearly 900,000 jobs. Because the accommodation of

Appendix Table II.4 SQUARE FEET PER EMPLOYEE CALCULATIONS

	Maisel[a]	Rosen[b]
1972	165.6	
1979	194.2	
1984		267.3 (boom)
1985		285.5
1986	229.4	281.0
1987		279.4
1988	236.1	282.8
1989		285.9
1990		287.5
1991		293.6 (recession)
Avg. 1985–90		283.7

a. Estimates in this column are from Maisel (1989).
b. Estimates in this column are based on Rosen's 1991 database for 67 metropolitan statistical areas (MSAs) across the country representing 2.2 billion square feet of space.

This appendix was prepared by Daniel T. Van Dyke.

Appendix Table II.5 SQUARE FEET PER EMPLOYEE: REGRESSION ESTIMATES

		Coefficient	Standard Error
With MSA dummies	Office employment	216	19.8
Without MSA dummies	Office employment	267	17.8
With MSA dummies	FIRE employment	251	26.6
	Services office employment	152	37.7
Without MSA dummies	FIRE employment	256	36.5
	Services office employment	275	28.7

Note: Regression estimates were pooled during 1984–90 from 67 metropolitan statistical areas (MSAs).

space to employment lags, during a boom the intensity coefficient will decline.

Conversely, 1991 was a recession year with office employment declining. Again because space accommodation for office employment lags changes in employment, the intensity coefficient rose in response to the recession. I do not necessarily believe that either the 1984 or 1991 data point represents an equilibrium desired stock of office space per employee. Rather, those data points contain a substantial component of undesired usage that will dissipate over the longer term. From 1985 to 1990, the (stock-weighted) average across the 67 metropolitan statistical areas (MSAs) was 283.7 square feet per office employee.

But even this number is likely an overestimate. From 1985 through 1991, the growth in office jobs declined steadily. As the growth of office employment slows, and the adjustment of space needs lags for more than a year, even the rather steady 283.7 square feet per employee will be high. Using statistical analysis, one can obtain yet another estimate of the space intensity of office employment. I analyzed the data by regressing the change in office employment on the net absorption of office space by MSA from 1984 to 1990, in a pooled sample from our database. I analyzed the data both with and without MSA-specific dummy variables. Appendix table II.5 shows the results of this analysis. In the first two rows, office employment was aggregated as the sum of finance, insurance, and real estate employment, as well as employment in the relevant service sectors. The regression with dummies yields a space intensity coefficient of 215 square feet per employee. The intercept can be roughly interpreted as the amount of space that is invariant with respect to employment, or the load factor. It also catches factors unique to the MSA that would not otherwise be captured. Thus, the 216 square feet per employee can be thought of as the unloaded demand for space per employee.

The regression without dummies yields a coefficient of space intensity of 267 square feet per employee. Because there is no intercept in this specification of the equation, the coefficient can be roughly interpreted as the fully loaded demand for space per employee. The ratio of 267 to 216 is 1.236; in other words, the load factor is estimated to be 23.6 percent. This estimate of the load factor corresponds very closely to commonly used rules of thumb in the industry of 15 percent to 20 percent. Thus, I am confident that the estimates derived here are not spurious.

REFERENCES

Alli, Kasim L., Gabriel G. Ramirez, and Kenneth Yung. 1991. "Corporate Headquarters Relocation: Evidence from the Capital Markets." *AREUEA Journal* 19(4, Winter): 583–99.

Anonymous. 1992. "The Rent Adjustment Process and the Structural Vacancy Rate in the Commercial Real Estate Market." Paper submitted through anonymous review process.

Archer, Wayne R. 1981. "Determinants of Location for General Purpose Office Firms within Medium Size Cities." *AREUEA Journal* 9(3, Fall): 283–97.

Armstrong, Regina Belz, and Boris Pushkarev. 1972. *The Office Industry: Patterns of Growth and Location.* Cambridge, Mass.: MIT Press.

Barth, James R., Michael D. Bradley, Joseph A. McKenzie, and G. Stacey Sirmans. 1988. "Stylized Facts about Housing and Construction Activity during the Post-World War II Period." In *Real Estate Market Analysis: Methods and Applications,* edited by J. M. Clapp and S. D. Messner (215–37). New York: Praeger Publishers.

Benjamin, John D., James D. Shilling, and C. F. Sirmans. 1992. "Security Deposits, Adverse Selection, and Office Leases." *AREUEA Journal* 20(2, Summer): 259–72.

Benjamin, John D., J. Sa-Aadu, and James D. Shilling. 1992. "Influence of Rent Differentials on the Choice between Office Rent Contracts with and without Relocation Provisions." *AREUEA Journal* 20(2, Summer): 289–302.

Berger, Jay S. 1968. *The Determination of the Economic Height of High-Rise Buildings.* Occasional Paper No. 3, Housing Real Estate and Urban Land Studies. Los Angeles: Graduate School of Management, University of California at Los Angeles.

Beyers, William B., and Michael J. Alvine. 1985. "Export Services in Post-Industrial Society." *Papers of the Regional Science Association* 57: 33–45.

Birch, David L. 1986. "America's Office Needs: 1985–1995." Chicago: Arthur Anderson & Co.

Brennan, Thomas P., Roger E. Cannaday, and Peter F. Colwell. 1984. "Office Rents in the Chicago CBD." *AREUEA Journal* 12(3, Fall): 243–60.

Burns, Leland S. 1977. "The Location of the Headquarters of Industrial Companies: A Comment." *Urban Studies* 14(June): 211–14.

Byrne, Therese E., and Sandon J. Goldberg. 1992. "London and Manhattan: Yield Playgrounds in 'Tried and True' Cities." New York: Salomon Brothers, United States Real Estate Research, U.S. Office Market, September.

Cannaday, Roger E., and Han Bin Kang. 1984. "Estimation of Market Rent for Office Space." *Real Estate Appraiser and Analyst* 50(2, Summer): 67–72.

Charles River Associates. 1981. "The Office Industry: Locational Patterns and Emerging Trends." CRA Report 424. Boston: Author, September.

Clapp, John M. 1980. "The Intrametropolitan Location of Office Activities." *Journal of Regional Science* 20(3): 387–99.

———. 1983. "A Model of Public Policy toward Office Relocation." *Environment and Planning, A* 15: 1299–1309.

———. 1988. "Empirical Analysis of Office Markets: An Evaluation of Interdisciplinary Research." Working Paper. Storrs, Conn.: Center for Real Estate and Urban Economic Studies.

———. 1989. "Absorption Forecasts Using Employment and Population Growth." In *Forecasting: Market Determinants Affecting Cash Flows and Reversions*, edited by Joy White (14–28). Chicago: American Institute of Real Estate Appraisers.

Clapp, John M., and Peter Dorpalen. 1989. "Comparison of Office Locations in Hartford and New Britain: An Analysis of Clerical and Administrative Support Employment." University of Connecticut, Storrs, August. Draft.

Clapp, John M., Henry O. Pollakowski, and Lloyd Lynford. 1992. "Intrametropolitan Location and Office Market Dynamics." *AREUEA Journal* 20(2, Summer): 229–58.

Code, W. R. 1979. "The Planned Decentralization of Offices in Toronto: A Dissenting View," Geographical Papers No. 42. London, Ontario: Department of Geography, University of Western Ontario, September.

———. 1983. "The Strength of the Centre: Downtown Offices and Metropolitan Decentralization Policy in Toronto." *Environment and Planning A* 15(10, October): 1361–80.

Coffey, W. J., and M. Polese. 1987. "Trade and Location of Producer Services: A Canadian Perspective." *Environment and Planning A* 19(5, May): 597–612.

Cowan, Peter, et al. 1969. *The Office: A Facet of Urban Growth.* London: Heinemann Publishers.

Cushman & Wakefield of Connecticut, Inc. 1991. "Hartford and New Haven Market Report, Year-End 1991." Author.

Daniels, Peter W. 1977. "Office Locations in the British Conurbations: Trends and Strategies." *Urban Studies* 14(October): 261–74.

――――. 1980. "Office Location and the Journey to Work." Liverpool: Gower.

――――. 1982. *Service Industries: Growth and Location.* Cambridge, England: Cambridge University Press.

――――. 1986. "Technology and Metropolitan Office Location." University of Liverpool, Liverpool, England. Draft.

Daniels, Peter W., Ed. 1979. *Spatial Patterns of Office Growth and Location.* Chichester, Sussex, England: John Wiley & Sons.

DiPasquale, Denise, and William C. Wheaton. 1992. "The Markets for Real Estate Assets and Space: A Conceptual Framework." *AREUEA Journal* 20(2, Summer): 181–98.

Doiron, John C., James D. Shilling, and C. F. Sirmans. 1992. "Do Market Rents Reflect the Value of Special Building Features?" *Journal of Real Estate Research* 7(2, Fall): 147–156.

Dokko, Yoon, and Robert H. Edelstein. 1992. "Towards a Real Estate Land Use Modeling Paradigm." *AREUEA Journal* 20(2, Summer): 199–210.

Downs, Anthony. 1986. "Why Haven't Office Building Prices Fallen More Sharply?" New York: Salomon Brothers, September.

Dunning, J. H., and G. Norman. 1987. "The Location Choice of Offices of International Companies." *Environment and Planning A* 19(5, May): 613–32.

Eubank, A. A., and C. F. Sirmans. 1979. "The Price Adjustment Mechanism for Rental Housing in the United States." *Quarterly Journal of Economics* 93(1): 163–83.

Evans, Alan W. 1973. "The Location of the Headquarters of Industrial Companies." *Urban Studies* 10(October): 387–95.

Farley Company. 1990. "Greater Hartford Office Market Report." Hartford: Author, Winter.

Fisher, Jeffrey D. 1992. "Integrating Research in Markets for Space and Capital." *AREUEA Journal* 20(2, Summer): 161–80.

Fisher, Jeffrey D., and R. Brian Webb. 1991. "Development of a National Lease Index for Commercial Real Estate." Indiana University, Bloomington. Draft.

————. 1992. "Current Issues in the Analysis of Commercial Real Estate." *AREUEA Journal* 20(2, Summer): 211–28.

————. 1993. "Development of an Effective Rent (Lease) Index for U.S. Office Space." Indiana University, Bloomington. Draft.

Fisher, Robert Moore. 1967. "The Boom in Office Buildings." Technical Bulletin 58. Washington, D.C.: Urban Land Institute.

Frydl, Edward J. 1991. *Overhangs and Hangovers: Coping with the Imbalances of the 1980s.* Annual Report of Federal Reserve Bank of New York. New York: Federal Reserve Bank of New York.

Gad, Gunter H. K. 1979. "Face-to-Face Linkages and Office Decentralization: A Study of Toronto." In *Spatial Patterns of Office Growth and Location,* edited by P. W. Daniels. Chichester, Sussex, England: John Wiley & Sons.

Gallie, William B. 1966. *Pierce and Pragmatism.* New York: Dover Publications.

Giliberto, S. Michael, and Bedford H. Lydon. 1993. "A Graphic History of U.S. Office Space Supply and Demand, 1972–92." New York: Salomon Brothers, United States Real Estate Research, February.

Glascock, John L., Shirin Jahanian, and C. F. Sirmans. 1990. "An Analysis of Office Market Rents: Some Empirical Evidence." *AREUEA Journal* 18(1, Spring): 105–119.

Goddard, John B. 1968. "Multivariate Analysis of Office Location Patterns in the City Centre: A London Example." *Regional Studies* 2: 69–85.

————. 1973. *Office Linkages and Location.* Oxford, England: Pergamon Press.

————. 1975. *Office Location in Urban and Regional Development* London: Oxford University Press.

Goddard, John B., and John N. Marshall. 1983. "The Future of Offices." In *The Future for the City Centre.* Institute of British Geographers.

Goddard, John B., and Diana Morris. 1976. *The Communications Factor in Office Decentralization.* Oxford, England: Pergamon Press.

Goldman-Sachs. 1986. *Real Estate Report* (Fall). New York: Author.

Gould, Stephen Jay. 1980. *The Panda's Thumb: More Reflections in Natural History.* New York: W. W. Norton & Co.

Graham, Lisa, and S. Michael Giliberto. 1993. "Altering Lease Flexibility with Cyclical Implications on Office Property Returns,"

New York: Salomon Brothers, United States Real Estate Research, April.

Guttentag, Jack M. 1992. "When Will Residential Mortgage Underwriting Come of Age?" *Housing Policy Debate* 3(1): 143–56.

Hamer, Andrew M. 1974. "Metropolitan Planning and the Location Behavior of Basic Office Firms: A Case Study," *Review of Regional Studies*, 4(suppl.): 34–45.

Hardman, Sir Henry. 1973. *The Dispersal of Government Work from London.* London: Her Majesty's Stationery Office, June.

Heilbrun, James. 1987. *Urban Economics and Public Policy.* New York: St. Martin's Press.

Hekman, John S. 1985. "Rental Price Adjustment and Investment in the Office Market." *AREUEA Journal* 13(1, Spring): 32–47.

Hendershott, Patric H., and Edward J. Kane. 1992. "Causes and Consequences of the 1980s Commercial Construction Boom." *Journal of Applied Corporate Finance* 5(1, Spring): 61–70.

Hough, Douglas E., and C. G. Kratz. 1983. "Can 'Good' Architecture Meet the Market Test?" *Journal of Urban Economics* 14(1, July): 40–54.

Ihlanfeldt, Keith R., and Michael D. Raper. 1990. "The Intrametropolitan Location of New Office Firms." *Land Economics* 66(2, May): 182–198.

Kelly, Hugh F. 1983. "Forecasting Office Space Demand in Urban Areas." *Real Estate Review* 13(3, Fall): 87–95.

Kling, John L., and Thomas E. McCue. 1987. "Office Building Investment and the Macroeconomy: Empirical Evidence, 1973–1985." *AREUEA Journal* 15(3, Fall): 234–55.

Kroll, Cynthia. 1984. "Employment Growth and Office Space along the 680 Corridor: Booming Supply and Potential Demand in a Suburban Area." Working Paper 84-75. Berkeley, Calif.: Center for Real Estate and Urban Economics, February.

Kutay, Aydan. 1986. "Optimum Office Location and the Comparative Statics of Information Economies." *Regional Studies* 20(6).

Lichtenberg, Robert M. 1960. *One-Tenth of a Nation.* Cambridge, Mass.: Harvard University Press.

Liu, Crocker H., David J. Hartzell, Terry V. Grissom, and Wylie Grieg. 1990. "The Composition of the Market Portfolio and Real Estate Investment Performance." *AREUEA Journal* 18(1, Spring): 49–75.

Long, Sharon Kay. 1984. "The Location of Office Activities: A Theoretical and Empirical Analysis." Ph.D. diss., University of North Carolina, Chapel Hill.

Long, Sharon K., Ann D. Witte, Helen Tauchen, and Wayne Archer. 1984. "The Location of Office Firms." University of North Carolina, School of Business, October. Draft.

Louargand, Marc Andrew. 1981. "Intrametropolitan Location of Office Activity," Ph.D. diss., University of California at Los Angeles.

Lydon III, Bedford H., and S. Michael Gilberto. 1993. "Lots of Pain, Little Gain." New York: Salomon Brothers, United States Real Estate Research, U.S. Office Markets, January.

Maisel, S. J. 1989. "Demand for Office Space." Working Paper 89–161. Berkeley, Calif.: Center for Real Estate and Urban Economics.

Margo, Robert A. 1992. "Explaining the Postwar Suburbanization of Population in the United States: The Role of Income." *Journal of Urban Economics* 31: 301–10.

Marshall, J. N. 1982. "Linkages between Manufacturing Industry and Business Services." *Environment and Planning A* 14(11, November): 1523–40.

———. 1983. "Business Service Activities in British Provincial Conurbations." *Environment and Planning A* 15(10, October): 1343–59.

Marshall, J. N., P. Damesick, and P. Wood. 1987. "Understanding the Location and Role of Producer Services in the United Kingdom." *Environment and Planning A* 19(5, May): 575–96.

Matrullo, Michael. 1979. "The Office Industry Survey, Part II: An Analysis of Office Tenant Responses." Boston: Boston Redevelopment Authority, March. Photocopy.

McIntosh, Willard, and Glenn V. Henderson, Jr. 1989. "Efficiency of the Office Properties Market." *Journal of Real Estate Finance and Economics* 2(1, February): 61–70.

Miles, Mike, Rebel Cole, and David Guilkey. 1990. "A Different Look at Commercial Real Estate Returns." *AREUEA Journal* 18(4, Winter): 403–30.

Miles, Mike, David Hartzell, David Guilkey, and D. Shears. 1991. "A Transactions-Based Real Estate Index: Is it Possible?" *Journal of Property Research* 8: 203–17.

Mills, Edwin S. 1992. "Office Rent Determinants in the Chicago Area." *AREUEA Journal* 20(2, Summer): 273–88.

Noyelle, Thierry J., and Thomas M. Stanback, Jr. 1984. *The Economic Transformation of American Cities.* Totowa, N.J.: Rowman and Allanhead.

Pascal, Anthony. 1987. "The Vanishing City." *Urban Studies* 24(6, December): 597–603.

Peddle, Michael T. 1987. "The Appropriate Estimation of Intrametropolitan Firm Location Models: An Empirical Note." *Land Economics* 63(3, August): 303–05.

Pollakowski, Henry, Susan Wachter, and Lloyd Lynford. 1992. "Did Office Market Size Matter in the 1980s? A Time-Series Cross-Sectional Analysis of Metropolitan Area Office Markets." *AREUEA Journal* 20(2, Summer): 303–24.

Price Waterhouse Real Estate Group. 1992. "The Downtown Los Angeles Office Market: Analysis of Historical Trends and Projections to the 1990s." Los Angeles: Author, April.

Pye, R. 1977. "Office Location and the Cost of Maintaining Contact." *Environment and Planning A* 9(2, February): 149–68.

Ragas, Wade R., Ronald C. Rogers, and John L. Hysom. 1991. "A Judgmental Model of Office Demand and Supply." University of New Orleans, January. Draft.

Ragas, Wade R., Robert L. Ryan, and Terry V. Grissom. 1992. "Forecasting Office Space Demand and Office Space per Worker Estimates." *SIOREF/Perspective* 51(2, Mar./Apr.): 2–8.

Rannels, John. 1956. *The Core of the City.* New York: Columbia University Press.

Raper, Michael D. 1988. "The Intrametropolitan Location of New Office Firms." Ph.D. diss., Georgia State University, Atlanta.

Rhodes, John, and Arnold Kan. 1971. *Office Dispersal and Regional Policy.* Cambridge, England: Cambridge University Press.

Robbins, Sidney M., and Nestor E. Terleckyj. 1960. *Money Metropolis.* Cambridge, Mass.: Harvard University Press.

Rosen, Kenneth T. 1984. "Toward a Model of the Office Building Sector." *AREUEA Journal* 12(3, Fall): 261–69.

Rosen, Kenneth T., and Lawrence B. Smith. 1983. "The Price-Adjustment Process for Rental Housing and the Natural Vacancy Rate." *American Economic Review* 83(4, September): 779–86.

Rosen, Sherwin. 1974. "Hedonic Prices and Implicit Markets." *Journal of Political Economy* 82: 33–55.

Schmenner, Roger W. 1991. "Service Sector Location Decision Making: Some Midwestern Evidence." Indiana University Business School, Bloomington. Draft.

Scott, A. J. 1983. "Location and Linkage Systems: A Survey and Reassessment." *Annals of Regional Science* 17(March): 1–39.

Shilling, James D., C. F. Sirmans, and John B. Corgel. 1987. "Price Adjustment Process for Rental Office Space." *Journal of Urban Economics* 22(1, July): 90–100.

———. 1992. "Natural Office Vacancy Rates: Some Additional Estimates." *Journal of Urban Economics* 31: 140–43.

Shilton, Leon. 1985. *Manhattan Office Industries and Office Space, 1970–1983.* New York: Sylvan Lawrence Research Center, New York University.

Short, John, Ederyn Williams, and Bruce Christie. 1976. *The Social Psychology of Telecommunications.* London: John Wiley & Sons.

Shulman, David, and Sandon J. Goldberg. 1992. "A Graphic History of U.S. Office Space Supply and Demand, 1972–91." New York: Salomon Brothers, United States Real Estate Research, U.S. Office Market, February.

Siegel, Jeremy J. 1991. "The Real Estate-Induced Recession." *Economic Outlook* (Wharton Real Estate Center, Philadelphia) 5(2, Late Summer): 2.

———. 1992. "This Long Recession Will Soon End." *Economic Outlook* (Wharton Real Estate Center, Philadelphia) 5(Spring): 4.

Smith, Randy W., and David Selwood. 1983. "Office Location and the Density Distance Relationship." *Urban Geography* 4(4): 302–16.

Stanback, Thomas M., Jr., and Richard V. Knight. 1970. *The Metropolitan Economy,* New York: Columbia University Press.

Thibodeau, Thomas G. 1990. "Estimating the Effect of High-Rise Office Buildings on Residential Property Values." *Land Economics* 66(4): 402–08.

Thorngren, B. 1970. "How Do Contact Systems Affect Regional Development?" *Environment and Planning* 2: 409–27.

Tornqvist, Gunnar. 1970. "Contact Systems and Regional Development." *Lund Studies in Geography,* ser. B, no. 35. Lund, Sweden: Royal University of Lund.

U.S. Department of Commerce, Bureau of Economic Analysis. 1985. *BEA Regional Projections.* Vol. 2 in Metropolitan Statistical Area Projections to 2035. Washington, D.C.: Author.

van Dinteren, J. H. J. 1987. "The Role of Business-Service Offices in the Economy of Medium-Sized Cities." *Environment and Planning A* 19(5, May): 669–86.

Vandell, Kerry D., Jonathan S. Lane. 1989. "The Economics of Architecture and Urban Design: Some Preliminary Findings." *AREUEA Journal* 17(2, Summer): 253–60.

Voith, Richard P. 1992. "A Note on Natural Office Vacancy Rates." *Journal of Urban Economics* 31: 138–39.

Voith, Richard, and Theodore Crone. 1988. "National Vacancy Rates and the Persistence of Shocks in U.S. Office Markets." *AREUEA Journal* 16(4, Winter): 437–58.

Wabe, J. S. 1966. "Office Decentralization: An Empirical Study." *Urban Studies* 3(February): 35–55.

Warf, Barney. 1989. "Telecommunications and the Globalization of Financial Services." *Professional Geographer* 41(3): 257–71.

Webb, R. Brian, and Jeffrey D. Fisher. 1993. "Development of an Effective Rent (Lease) Index for the Chicago CBD." Indiana University, Bloomington. Draft.

Webb, R. Brian, Mike Miles, and David Guilkey. 1992. "Transactions-Driven Commercial Real Estate Returns: The Panacea to Asset Allocation Models?" *AREUEA Journal* 20(2, Summer): 325 ff.

Wheaton, William C. 1984. "The Incidence of Interjurisdictional Differences in Commercial Property Taxes." *National Tax Journal* 37(4, December): 515–27.

_____. 1987. "The Cyclic Behavior of the National Office Market." *AREUEA Journal* 15(4, Winter): 281–99.

_____. 1990. "Vacancy, Search, and Prices in a Housing Market Matching Model." *Journal of Political Economy* 98(6): 1990.

Wheaton, William C., and Denise DiPasquale. Forthcoming. *Real Estate Economics.* Englewood Cliffs, N.J.: Prentice-Hall.

Wheaton, William C., and Raymond Torto. 1985. "The National Office Market: History and Future Prospects II." Boston: Center for Real Estate Development, Massachusetts Institute of Technology, February.

_____. 1988. "Vacancy Rates and the Future of Office Rents." *AREUEA Journal* 16(4, Winter): 430–36.

_____. 1992. "Office Rent Indices and Their Behavior Over Time." Center for Real Estate, Massachusetts Institute of Technology, Boston, January. Draft.

Wilson, Mark I., and Sharmistha Bagchi-Sen. 1990. "The Determinants and Consequences of the Offshore Location of Services." Michigan State University, East Lansing. Draft.

John M. Clapp is professor in the department of finance, University of Connecticut, where he teaches real estate market analysis and other courses related to real estate and finance. His work has focused on the location of office buildings, office market analysis, cycles in regional employment growth, the appraisal of special purpose properties, mortgage underwriting and the design of adjustable rate mortgages. Professor Clapp has published extensively in the *Journal of Regional Science*, the *AREUEA Journal*, the *Journal of Urban Economics*, *The Quarterly Journal of Economics*, *The Journal of the American Statistical Association*, and other journals. He is on the editorial boards of the *AREUEA Journal*, *The Journal of Real Estate Finance and Economics* and the *Journal of Regional Science*. In 1987 he published the *Handbook for Real Estate Market Analysis* with Prentice Hall.

ABOUT THE COMMENTATORS

Kenneth T. Rosen is professor of business administration and chairman of the Center for Real Estate and Urban Economics at the University of California at Berkeley. He specializes in real estate economics and finance and has written more than 75 articles and papers, four books, and dozens of consulting reports. His most recent book, *Affordable Housing: New Policies for the Housing and Mortgage Markets,* provides detailed data and forecasts on mortgage and housing markets. Dr. Rosen is president of the Rosen Consulting Group, which specializes in tracking real estate markets in the top 67 markets in the country. He is on the boards of many private corporations and federal and state agencies dealing with real estate finance and development.

Michael Raper is assistant professor of economics and holder of the Sewell Chair of Private Enterprise at West Georgia College. He was formerly a senior research associate at Research Atlanta where he published a monograph on the effect of suburban office development on downtown Atlanta's office market. His current research interests are interurban cost-of-living differentials and regressivity in residential property tax assessments.

Keith Ihlanfeldt is professor of economics and senior research associate in the Policy Research Center at Georgia State University. His research has focused on a wide range of urban problems, including discrimination in the housing and labor markets, urban poverty, neighborhood decline, and housing affordability. He is currently studying the growth in income inequality within metropolitan areas. He has published numerous journal articles and his book, *Job Accessibility and the Employment and School Enrollment of Teenagers,* has recently been published by the W. E. Upjohn Institute for Employment Research.

ABOUT THE INSTITUTIONS

**THE AMERICAN REAL ESTATE AND URBAN ECONOMICS ASSO-
CIATION (AREUEA)** was organized at the 1964 meeting of the Allied
Social Science Associations in Chicago. AREUEA grew from the dis-
cussions of individuals who recognized a need for more information
and analysis in the fields of real estate development, planning, and
economics. Events since that time have more than justified the con-
cerns felt by the founders of AREUEA. The continuing efforts of the
association have advanced the scope of knowledge in these disciplines, and have facilitated the exchange of information and opinions
among academic, professional, and governmental people who are
concerned with urban economics and real estate issues.

Specifically, the purposes of AREUEA are to promote education
and encourage research in real estate, urban economics, and related
areas; to improve communication and exchange of information in
real estate, urban economics, and allied areas among college and
university faculty members; and to facilitate the association of academic, practicing professional, and research persons in real estate,
urban economics, and allied areas.

THE URBAN INSTITUTE is a nonprofit research and educational
organization established in Washington, D.C., in 1968. Its staff investigates the social and economic problems confronting the nation and
public and private means to alleviate them. The Urban Institute has
three goals for its research and dissemination activities: to sharpen
thinking about societal problems and efforts to solve them, to improve
government decisions and performance, and to increase citizen
awareness of important public choices.

Through work that ranges from broad conceptual studies to administrative and technical assistance, Institute researchers contribute to
the stock of knowledge and the analytic tools available to guide
decision making in the public interest.

The Institute disseminates its research and the research of others
through the publications program of it Press.

ABOUT THE SERIES

The American Real Estate And Urban Economics Association (AREUEA) was organized in 1964 based on the felt need to improve information and analysis in the fields of real estate development, planning, and urban economics. The AREUEA Monograph Series is designed to provide teachers, students, and practitioners with a comprehensive and timely presentation of recent research materials translated into summary form, which is more quickly and easily comprehended than journal articles and specialized studies. These monographs review old views, new techniques, and recent data. They should be particularly useful as supplements to classroom instruction or continuing professional education of practitioners.

Development of the AREUEA Monographs is supervised by a committee appointed by the AREUEA Board of Directors. In order to insure balanced coverage, outside commentators are invited to provide suggestions for revision to the author and to add brief comments on elements of the literature which supplement the body of the monograph. For this first monograph, Michael Raper and Keith Ihlanfeldt have written one commentary, Kenneth Rosen has provided the other.

The AREUEA Monograph Committee:
Anthony M.J. Yezer, Series Editor
George Washington University

Patric H. Hendershott
Ohio State University

David Ling
University of Florida

James D. Shilling
University of Wisconsin